# HORACE

## The Complete Odes and Epodes
## with the Centennial Hymn

TRANSLATED, WITH NOTES, BY W. G. SHEPHERD

WITH AN INTRODUCTION BY BETTY RADICE

D0111120

PENGUIN BOOKS

## PENGUIN BOOKS

Published by the Penguin Group
Penguin Books Ltd, 80 Strand, London WC2R 0RL, England
Penguin Putnam Inc., 375 Hudson Street, New York, New York 10014, USA
Penguin Books Australia Ltd, Ringwood, Victoria, Australia
Penguin Books Canada Ltd, 10 Alcorn Avenue, Toronto, Ontario, Canada M4V 3B2
Penguin Books India (P) Ltd, 11 Community Centre, Panchsheel Park, New Delhi – 110 017, India
Penguin Books (NZ) Ltd, Cnr Rosedale and Airborne Roads, Albany, Auckland, New Zealand
Penguin Books (South Africa) (Pty) Ltd, 24 Sturdee Avenue, Rosebank 2196 South Africa

Penguin Books Ltd, Registered Offices: 80 Strand, London WC2R 0RL, England

www.penguin.com

This translation first published 1983
26

Printed in England by Clays Ltd, St Ives plc
Set in Linotron Bembo

www.greenpenguin.co.uk

Penguin Books is committed to a sustainable
future for our business, our readers and our
planet. This book is made from paper certified
by the Forest Stewardship Council.

# THE COMPLETE ODES AND EPODES

ADVISORY EDITOR: BETTY RADICE

QUINTUS HORATIUS FLACCUS was born in late 65 B.C. at Venusia in Apulia. His father, though once a slave, had made enough money as an auctioneer to send his son to well-known teachers in Rome and subsequently to the university at Athens. There Horace joined Brutus's army and served on his staff until the defeat at Philippi in 42 B.C. On returning to Rome, he found that his father was dead and his property had been confiscated, but he succeeded in obtaining a secretarial post in the treasury, which gave him enough to live on. The poetry he wrote in the next few years impressed Virgil, who introduced him to the great patron Maecenas in 38 B.C. This event marked the beginning of a life-long friendship. From now on Horace had no financial worries; he moved freely among the leading poets and statesmen of Rome; his work was admired by Augustus, and indeed after Virgil's death in 19 B.C. he was virtually Poet Laureate. Horace died in 8 B.C., only a few months after Maecenas.

W. G. SHEPHERD was born in Kent in 1935. He was educated at Brentwood School and Jesus College, Cambridge, where he read the English tripos, graduating in 1958. During National Service he was commissioned in the Royal Artillery. Nowadays he lives at Southgate, in North London, with his wife, daughter and two sons, and in 1991 retired from working as a contracts executive in a major electronics firm. He plays the piano and clavichord a great deal – mainly late baroque and classical music. Four volumes of his poetry have been published: *Sun, Oak, Almond, I* (1970), *Evidences* (1980), *Self-Love* (1982) and *The First Zone of the Growth Furnace* (1984). His translation of Propertius's Poems was published in the Penguin Classics series in 1985.

BETTY RADICE read classics at Oxford, then married and, in the intervals of bringing up a family, tutored in classics, philosophy and English. She became joint editor of the Penguin Classics in 1964. As well as editing the translation of Livy's *The War with Hannibal* she translated Livy's *Rome and Italy*, the Latin comedies of Terence, Pliny's *Letters*, Erasmus's *Praise of Folly* and *The Letters of Abelard and Heloise* for the Penguin Classics. She edited and introduced Edward Gibbon's *Memoirs of My Life* for the Penguin English Library, edited and annotated her translation of the younger Pliny's works for the Loeb Library of Classics, and translated from Italian, Renaissance Latin and Greek for the Officina

Bodoni of Verona. She collaborated as a translator in the Collected Works of Erasmus in preparation by the University of Toronto, edited an eight-volume production of Gibbon's *Decline and Fall of the Roman Empire* for the Folio Society, and compiled the Penguin Reference Book *Who's Who in the Ancient World*. Betty Radice, who was an honorary fellow of St Hilda's College, Oxford, and a vice-president of the Classical Association, died in 1985.

*For Michael Benson and Peter Whigham*

# CONTENTS

Introduction                                    9
Select Bibliography                            39
Translator's Foreword                          41

Epodes                                         45
Odes, Book I                                   67
Odes, Book II                                 103
Odes, Book III                               127
Centennial Hymn                              165
Odes, Book IV                                171

Appendix: Suetonius,
    The Life of Horace                       194
Notes                                        197
Glossary of Proper Names                     227
Index to Poems                               251

# INTRODUCTION

It is unfashionable today to look into a poet's background to gain a better appreciation of his poetry; and yet such places as Rydal Water, Laugharne, the Lincolnshire wolds, and Oxford – still branchy between towers in spite of an increasingly base and brickish skirt – gave something to their poets to carry through life and to influence their writing. The difficulty with the poets of ancient Greece and Rome is that, more often than not, we simply do not know enough about them as individuals to be able to guess at the influences at work on them, possibly because they chose to tell us little or nothing. *Sulmo mihi patria est,* wrote Ovid, and his statue stands in modern Sulmona; but Rome, not the Abruzzi, was his spiritual home. Juvenal too was evidently quick to leave his native Aquinum in Volscian country for all that Rome could offer him. Mantuan Virgil is, of course, one exception; another is Horace, about whom we know a good deal. Horace enjoyed writing about himself, either quite factually in his longer conversational poems, or in teasing hints in his lyric odes. Three places move in and out of his poetry: the small provincial town in southern Italy where he spent his early childhood; Rome at a time of political upheaval and literary activity; and his refuge from the pressures of urban life – the villa and small farm he owned in the pleasantly wooded Sabine hills not far from modern Tivoli.

Horace fixes the date of his birth himself in addressing his faithful wine-jar 'that was born like me when Manlius was consul' (III.21). Lucius Manlius Torquatus and Lucius Cotta were consuls in 66–65 B.C. The *Life of Horace* which Suetonius included in his biographies of the poets adds the day: 8 December.[1] His father was a freed slave who had worked as a *coactor*, an auctioneer's broker or assistant, and retired to Venusia (Venosa), a small settlement of ex-soldiers in Apulia down near the heel of Italy. Like many of us lucky enough to be born in a region of character, Horace never lost the feeling that this was where he belonged. He is 'a son of Lucania – or is it Apulia? For the settler at Venusia ploughs on the border of both' (*Satires* II.1.34–5).[2] There the 'familiar hills' of Apulia are 'scorched as usual by the Scirocco', which Horace calls by its regional name, Atabulus (*Satires* I.5.77–8); there he was 'born by sounding Aufidus' (IV.9.2), the river Ofanto, which provides the powerful simile of *Odes* IV.14.25–8:

> As bullish Aufidus rolls on,
> flowing by the realms of Apulian Daunus,
> and rages and threatens the cultivated fields
> with horrifying floods . . .

One of his grand Pindaric odes (III.4) moves straight from an invocation of the Muse Calliope to the poet's childhood in the Muses' special care:

> On pathless Vultur, beyond the threshold
> of my nurse Apulia, when I was exhausted
> with play and oppressed with sleep,
> legendary wood-doves once wove for me
>
> new-fallen leaves, to be
> a marvel to all who lodge in lofty
> Acherontia's eyrie and Bantia's woodlands
> and the rich valley farms of Forentum . . .

As Fraenkel remarks (*Horace*, p. 274), the three townlets named were 'presumably unknown to anyone who had not lived in that

---

1. See *Appendix*, p.194.
2. All translations quoted of the *Satires* and *Epistles* are by Niall Rudd.

far-off part of Italy'. And in the coda to *Odes* III his confidence in his 'monument more lasting than bronze' shows him as a prophet expecting honour in his own country:

> Where churning Aufidus resounds, where Daunus
> poor in water governed his rustic people,
> I shall be spoken of as one who was princely
> though of humble birth, the first to have brought
> Greek song into Latin numbers.

Horace mentions no other relative, not even his mother, but in *Satires* I.6 he pays tribute, in terms both affectionate and unsentimental, to his father, who thought the local school not good enough for his gifted son, and evidently wanted to remove him from the snobbery of the freeborn centurions' sons:

> He was a poor man with a few
> scraggy acres, yet he wouldn't send me to Flavius' school
> where the important boys, the sons of important sergeant-majors,
> used to go, with satchel and slate swinging from the left arm,
> clutching their tenpenny fee on the Ides of every month.
> Instead he courageously took his boy to Rome . . .

Horace writes with feeling; here perhaps is a childhood humiliation remembered over the years.

In Rome he had the best teachers, including Orbilius, who thrashed Livius Andronicus' Latin version of the *Odyssey* into his pupils, unaware that he would be immortalized as *plagosus* (*Epistles* II.1.70). He would also study rhetoric and Greek, which as a southern Italian he must have known to some extent already. Again he writes affectionately of the father who escorted him through the streets as his *paedagogus*, taking the opportunity to point out as warnings or examples the persons they met. 'And so he would talk my young character into shape' (*Satires* I.4.120), and awake the boy's interest in the quirks of human nature that he retained for life. After school came a university education, which for young Romans meant Athens:

> I had the luck to be raised in Rome, where I learned from my
>     teacher
> how much harm was done to the Greeks by the wrath of Achilles.

A little more was added in the way of a liberal training
by Athens; there I was keen to distinguish straight from crooked
and to go in search of truth among the Academy's trees.
                              (*Epistles* II.2.41–5)

All this ended after Julius Caesar was murdered in March 44 B.C.
At the end of August Brutus arrived in Athens. There, says
Plutarch (*Brutus*, 24), he attended lectures at the Academy, dis-
cussed philosophy, 'and appeared to be completely engrossed in
literary pursuits. But all this while, without anyone suspecting it,
he was making preparations for war . . . and at the same time he
rallied to his cause all the young Romans who were studying in
Athens.' One of them was Horace, aged not quite twenty-one, and
for the first time not under the watchful eye of his father. There is
no suggestion that, like Cicero's son, he had any strong political
feeling against tyranny; he is more likely to have joined Brutus on
romantic impulse or simply to go along with his fellow-students.
He followed his hero to Asia Minor, and by the time of the fighting
at Philippi he had been made a military tribune – one of six young
officers in temporary command of a legion, as an emergency
measure in the battle – despite his humble origins and lack of
experience. At the second battle, in November 42 B.C., Brutus was
defeated and killed himself, and Horace fled with the remnants of
the army. He says nothing of how he escaped, only that he threw
away his shield. If that is literally meant it would be practical, for a
shield could only slow down a man running for his life; but it
would be recognized by any educated audience of his poetry as a
familiar motif. The Greek lyric poets, Archilochus, Alcaeus and
possibly Anacreon, had all said the same of themselves.
    The shield discarded is a symbol of cowardice, and it marks
something which Horace might well have put aside as part of a
youthful episode in his life which was best forgotten. Instead, his
failure on the losing side and his loyalty to the leaders (who were
defeated but held to the ideals they fought for) keeps recurring; for
instance, he never loses his admiration for Cato. The defeat at
Philippi in a sense marks the end of Horace's youth; the army of
Brutus and Cassius was the last to fight with liberty as its cause. It
is touched on like a raw nerve in a brief mention in line 25 of III.4
('the broken line at Philippi'), and prompts one of the most

delicately tactful of the Odes (II.7), the welcome to an unknown friend who had not fled from the battlefield but retained his loyalty to the lost republican cause and gone on to fight for Pompey's nephew, Sextus Pompeius:

> O my friend and oldest comrade . . .

> . . . so often led with me
> into extremity by our general
> Brutus; who has restored you
> to citizenship, your native

> Gods and Italian skies? With you I knew
> the rout at Philippi and my shield,
> to my shame, left behind
> where manhood failed and words

> were eaten. Luckily Mercury
> bore me away, in my fright, in a cloud:
> but the undertow sucked you back
> to the weltering straits of war.

The mock-heroic reference to his rescue by Mercury, in the style of a Homeric hero, is wholly characteristic of Horace's ironic self-depreciation; but it does not mask the sense of personal inadequacy revived by thoughts of Philippi.

Once back in Italy, with his wings clipped, as he says himself (*Epistles* II.2.50), his father apparently dead, and his modest patrimony of house and farmland in Venusia confiscated, Horace took to writing verse to make a living, or rather to invite a patron to support him. More solid remuneration came from the post he obtained after the amnesty of 39 B.C. From the Suetonian *Life* we know that he became a clerk to the quaestors in the Treasury, which was also a record office, where State documents were copied and stored. The work may not have been arduous and could have been delegated; he seems still to have been holding it several years later, when *Satires* II.6 was written.

His position was radically changed when Maecenas, a wealthy, cultivated *eques* and personal adviser to the emperor, offered him patronage on the recommendation of the poets Virgil and Varius, and presented him with an estate and farm in the Sabine hills, in the

valley of the Digentia (now Licenza), some fourteen miles beyond
Tibur (Tivoli)[3] :

> This is what I prayed for. A piece of land – not so very big,
> with a garden and, near the house, a spring that never fails,
> and a bit of wood to round it off. All this and more
> the gods have granted.
>
> *(Satires* II.6.1–4)

In about 35 B.C. he published his first book of ten Satires, *saturae* or
miscellanies, for which the model was the Roman Gaius Lucilius,
the metre that of the standard Latin hexameter, and the subject the
faults and follies of man. Horace himself refers to them as *sermones*
– a term which aptly describes their easy conversational flow. All
ten poems are dedicated to Maecenas, and are presumably the ones
chosen for publication out of a wider range of *sermones* which had
been made known by public readings; *Satires* I.4 is written in
self-defence against accusations of personal malice and suggests
that Horace was already known for this kind of verse.

At the same time he must have been working on the early
Epodes; a collection of seventeen was published in 31 B.C. The
name is Greek, derived from *epōdos stichos*, the shorter line of an
iambic couplet. Horace always calls them his *iambi*.

> I was the first to show
> the iambics of Paros to Latium, keeping Archilochus' rhythms
> and fire, but not his themes or the words which hunted Lycambes.
>
> *(Epistles* I.19.23–5)

Here Horace is claiming (as he is later to claim for the greater
metrical variety of the Odes) that he is introducing something
quite new into Latin verse, namely the iambic metre of Archi-
lochus of Paros. There is too little surviving of Archilochus' poetry
for us to make a fair comparison: Fraenkel (p.27 ff.) quotes a
passage as a source for the tenth epode only to show the difference
between its fierce invective and Horace's literary adaptation,
which was not directed against any unfortunate Lycambes. This is
not unlike his extended use of Lucilius as a model for the Satires.

---

3. See Gilbert Highet, *Poets in a Landscape* pp.121–6 and Giuseppe Lugli, *La Villa
d'Orazio nella valle del Licenza*.

Possibly Horace's debt is no greater than that of Virgil to Theocritus in his pastoral poems; the tone can often be more like that of Hellenistic epigram.

The ten years between Philippi and Actium had been politically disturbed; first by the proscriptions of republicans, the last fling of the army at Utica, and the continued resistance of Sextus Pompeius, who was not finally defeated until 36 B.C.; and then by the growing tension between Octavian and Mark Antony which culminated in open rupture in 32 and declaration of war on Egypt, and ended with the victory at Actium (in 31 B.C.) and the capture of Alexandria. Some of the Epodes reflect these troubled times. Epode 7, on the suicidal civil wars in Rome, was probably written between 38 and 36; 16, perhaps Horace's first wholly serious poem, was inspired either by the Perusine War of 41 or, more probably, by a renewed outbreak of war with Sextus Pompeius in 38; for the first time Horace speaks of himself as an inspired prophet, a *vates* haranguing an imagined assembly of the Roman people and urging them to escape to the mythical Islands of the Blest. His vision owes something to Virgil's fourth Eclogue, already published in 40, and the description of the toil-free bounty of nature is rich in loving detail:

> where every year the earth, untilled, yields corn;
> and the vines, unpruned, forever bloom;
> and the never failing sprigs of olive bud;
> and dusky figs adorn their trees;
> and honey drips from the hollow oak; and the stream
> with plashing feet leaps lightly down from the lofty crag . . .

Epodes 1 and 9 are both addressed to Maecenas, the first reflecting Horace's anxiety and devotion to his friend about to take part in the engagement at Actium, the other evidently written when reports of the sea-battle and Cleopatra's defeat were encouraging but victory was not yet certain. It is interesting here to see Horace ignoring possible criticism. By the time the Epodes were published it was common knowledge that Maecenas did not, after all, join Octavian on this historic occasion.

Yet we may wonder how far Horace's deeper feelings were involved in several of these poems. We cannot expect the youthful intensity of Catullus; at thirty-four Horace was no angry young man – he was securely settled under a wealthy and sympathetic patron, and the author of a successful book published some four years previously. Very few of the Epodes can be dated, and the majority offer wit and elegance rather than personal sentiment: the diatribe against garlic (3); the attack on the swaggering upstart (4); the 'cowardly cur' (6); the harsh ill-wishes (10) to the Maevius who may be the poetaster of Virgil's *Eclogues* 3.90, and for which the Greek model referred to above marks the contrast between its own fierce personal note and Horace's professional expertise. Two brutally obscene taunts (8 and 12) are directed against ageing women still looking for lovers – a standard theme in antiquity. The late epode 14 is no more than a graceful apology to Maecenas for the book's being behind schedule because of a love-affair with 'the promiscuous ex-slave Phryne', but, in 11, the feeling 'sounds genuine, a vivid picture of the misery, helplessness and loss of self-respect that may torment the lover'.[4] The Neaera of 15 is presumably a pseudonym, following the convention Horace will adopt throughout the Odes, but there is more raw emotion here than Horace will often allow himself to show – no urbanity or ironic detachment, only a bitter jealousy which might be voiced by Catullus or Propertius:

> – And you, whoever you are, who amble
> happy and proud in my misfortune,
> though perhaps you are rich in flocks
> and land and Pactolus flows for you alone
> and Pythagoras' reincarnations pose
> no problems for you and your beauty
> surpasses that of Nireus, alas,
> you shall bewail her favours transferred
> to another, and I shall laugh last.

One name stands out as a personality: the witch Canidia is a fearsome figure. She is named in epode 3 and vividly portrayed and cursed by her child victim in 5, while in 17 she is treated to an ironic recantation by the poet, to which she replies with unrelenting fury. Canidia (with her ally Sagana) appears in the graveyard orgies of *Satires* I.8, and is named as a poisoner in *Satires* II.1.48 and in the

---

4. L. P. Wilkinson, *Horace and his Lyric Poetry*, p.46.

final line of II.8 ('Canidia, whose breath is more deadly than an African snake's'). She is identified by the scholiast Porphyrio as Gratidia, a Neapolitan sorceress and poisoner. This cannot be confirmed, but the way in which she haunts Horace's earlier poems suggests that she has some basis in reality.

The eight *sermones* of Book II of the Satires were published at about the same time, in 30 B.C., and after that Horace moved away from the genre of social commentary into what was to establish him as a lyric poet. Three books of *carmina*, eighty-eight lyric poems of widely varying style and length, appeared only seven years later; some of them must have been written while he was completing the Epodes. Indeed, there are two poems in the early collection which point so clearly forward that they cannot be classed as experimental. Epode 2 dwells on the simple life of the farmer in nostalgic detail – for farming was not really like that in Horace's own day – a theme which will often recur with the same delicate sentiment. It should not seem false here because of the mocking irony of the last five lines which bring us down to earth before we can float away into rosy sentimentality:

> – Thus Alfius, a moneylender,
> on the point of turning farmer:
> he called in all his capital
> on the Ides, and on the Kalends
> he's busily loaning it out again.

This was a device copied from Archilochus. The change of mood is very Horatian, as is the withholding of the true identity of the speaker until the end. Finally, epode 13 is close in spirit to *Odes* I.9, where 'A violent tempest narrows the heaven' or 'the trees cannot bear/their loads and bitter frosts/have paralysed the streams'. The poet tells us to shut out our cares with the comfort of good wine by a blazing fire. Then we are lifted into the wider context of the heroic age by the centaur Chiron singing of 'wine and song,/sweet ministration to ugly hurts', to Achilles, mortal son of an immortal mother, who cannot escape his destiny and will not live to return home. In such a context Lord Lytton wrote:

When a proper name is thus used – a proper name suggesting of itself almost insensibly to the mind the poetic associations which belong to the name – the idea is enlarged from a simple to a complex idea, adorned with delicate enrichments, and opening into many dim recesses of imagination.[5]

The first three books of the Odes are so richly varied in style and subject that they are difficult to classify. They are not arranged either by theme or chronology, the *persona* of the poet or the interests of the patron, though they start with an address to Maecenas ('descended from olden kings,/my rampart and sweet admiration') and end with a similar address in III.29 (III.30 being the coda to the whole collection).

In the first poem Horace sets himself above ordinary men by his devotion to the Muses:

> and should you list me among the lyric bards
> I shall nudge the stars with my lifted head.

In the coda he celebrates his achievement as the first to introduce Greek metres into Latin verse. He was not literally the first. Ennius had adapted the Greek hexameter to early accentual Latin; the dramatists Plautus and Terence had taken the iambics of Greek New Comedy for their model, and Terence claimed creative originality in doing so; two of Catullus' extant poems (11 and 51) are closely imitative of Sappho. But just as Horace had re-created the iambics of Archilochus in the Epodes, he now extended his range to the elaborate metres of the lyric poets of Lesbos, Alcaeus and Sappho; to Anacreon, Simonides and Stesichorus, and to the Hellenistic poets who in their turn had been influenced by the early lyricists. For his lofty poetic themes he looked to Bacchylides and Pindar. But Horace is no slavish imitator. His complex measures are creative modifications of his equally complex Greek models in order to suit the Latin language, and his mastery of his technique is complete. His pride in this, shown too in *Epistles* I:19, is very proper in a great poet who knows his capabilities.

What survives of Greek lyric poetry is sadly fragmentary, so that its influence on Horace cannot be as closely traced as one would like. Sometimes light is thrown on a puzzling poem by analogy with a known fragment: I.28, for instance, where it is a surprise to find half-way through that the dead mathematician Archytas is

5. Introduction to *The Odes of Horace*.

addressed by a drowned sailor, is paralleled by passages from Simonides of Ceos.[6] In III.4 the Muse is hailed in terms used by Pindar in *Pythians* I.1. On the other hand, the scholiast Porphyrio says explicitly that I.27 is taken from Anacreon's third book, but the surviving fragments of this (43D) are in a different metre, and the connection is probably no more than that of the plea for less riotous behaviour in Horace's first two stanzas. It would have been impossible anyway for Horace to have re-created the atmosphere of the Greek lyricists. Alcaeus and Sappho write very personally, Alcaeus in particular as an aristocratic opponent of the reigning tyrants of Lesbos. Their poems were sung to the lyre, while for Horace the lyre is a poetic convention. Their audiences were limited to a small social circle, and through their poetry they spoke in their own voices. So too did Catullus speak, and even more so Virgil and Lucretius, with single-minded purpose.

But Horace offers an elusive variety by assuming a wide range of poetic *personae*. He can speak now as the Muses' priest, the inspired follower of Bacchus, the immortal bard, and then be gently chiding some wayward girl in almost avuncular terms; he is the wryly humorous man of forty of whom lovers need not be jealous, and then he is himself a lover locked out. Sometimes he seriously attacks the social evils and insecurity of his times, the decay of family life, the overspending and overbuilding, and then he escapes to his country retreat to enjoy the good things of life – while they last, for his mood quickly shifts to the inevitability of approaching death. He is at once the loyal friend to the companions of his republican youth, the grateful admirer of Maecenas and Agrippa, the supporter of Augustus' measures to restore political stability to Rome, and the self-sufficient individualist who can still enjoy taking part in a simple rustic festival for the gods of rural Italy.

As with the *personae*, so with the localities from which Horace addresses his audience. In some of the Odes we are firmly in Rome, addressing individual Romans, as in the Satires; we see the wealthy building their grand houses in the City or their villas at Baiae, the drinking parties and the young men riding in the Campus Martius or swimming in the Tiber, the girls peeping out of doorways, and the 'lonely crone in an alley'. More often the scene moves to Tibur

6. See references in Wilkinson, pp. 109 ff.

or the Sabine farm with all the pleasures of the simple life. But frequently the poems are not localized at all: Greek and Roman elements are interwoven as are Greek and Roman proper names, and this has the liberating effect of taking the poem out of a factual context into a commentary on the human condition. Indeed, perhaps too much editorial effort has been applied to pinpointing a time and place. Take the famous I.9 ('See how Soracte stands deep/in dazzling snow . . .'); for Wilkinson (p. 130), Mount Soracte is local colour and the whole scene symbolic of old age. For Fraenkel (p. 176) the poem 'is dear to many of us primarily because it reminds us of the days when, either from a *terrazzo* on the roof of one of the tall and weathered houses off the Corso or from the height of the Gianicolo, we gazed at the queer silhouette which the isolated sharp peak of Monte Soratte forms against the northern horizon'. For West (p.6) the scene is set at Thaliarchus' home somewhere in the country from where Soracte can be seen in the near distance. Fraenkel finds that the combination of a wintry beginning (based on Alcaeus) and a summery ending means that the poem 'falls short of the perfection reached by Horace in many of his odes'. Yet others can see the perfect link in 'this is your green time, not your white/and morose' – salad days for the enjoyment of summer nights; and Wilkinson is surely right when he sees how the third stanza unites the poem 'if we feel the storm to be the storm of life, and the calm the calm of death'.

Horace also makes use of mythology to establish an individual ode in a general context. The 'grey wolf loping down from Lanuvium' on the Appian Way gives a Roman setting to Galatea's impending journey across the stormy Adriatic in III.27, but what remains with the reader is the transfer to a grand-style treatment of Europa's destined journey with Jove. In III.11 Mercury is asked to bring all his persuasive powers to bear on Lyde – powers which can comfort even the Danaids in hell, so that mention of their name carries us on to the noble refusal of Hypermnestra. (See Lord Lytton's comment quoted on pp. 17–18.) History is freely used in the same way, the expanded episode being either from the distant past (Regulus and the quiet heroism of his self-sacrifice in III.5) or one taken from the recent political turmoil. Thus in I.37 ('Friends, now is the time to drink') the celebration of the victory of Actium is less important than Cleopatra's fortitude:

resolved for death, she was brave indeed.
She was no docile woman but truly scorned
to be taken away in her enemy's ships,
deposed, to an overweening Triumph.

   Though it is so hard to fit the Odes into categories, there are
about twenty in Books I to III which can be called symposium
(drinking-party) poems, on the Greek model; here too their origi-
nality and often their depth rest on Horace's expanded treatment of
the type. The girls are always Greek, while the young men may be
Greek or Roman; rustic festivals are likely to be Italian, and the
gods have Greek attributes. Only rarely is an actual drinking-party
taking place, and the wine may be Greek ('of Lesbos' in I.17) or
Roman, 'put up to bask in smoke' from Horace's own vintage
(III.8), in Greek jars, 'a modest Sabine wine', no choice Caecuban
or Falernian (I.20). Often the symposium features only in the
initial request to a girl to make preparations or to a friend to accept
an invitation, before the poem moves on to its true purpose. One
ode (III.29) opens with a plea to Maecenas to leave the crowds and
smoke of Rome in the unhealthy season and shed his cares of State
for 'a jar of smooth wine as yet untilted', but the real message is
that

> Wisely the God enwraps in fuliginous night
> the future's outcome, and laughs
> if mortals are anxious beyond
> mortality's bound . . .

The future may be stormy, but the self-sufficient man may enjoy
the present and say,

> 'I have lived: tomorrow the Father
> may fill the vault with dark clouds
>
> or brilliant sunlight, but he will not render
> the past invalid, will not re-shape
> and make undone whatever
> the fleeting hour has brought.'

He can easily dispense with Fortune's gifts and 'pay court to honest
Poverty'; not for him to risk his life at sea for valuable cargo – he

takes to his dinghy before the storm. Here, as in similar poems, Horace neatly sums up his whole philosophy of life.

The Greek form of prayer or invocation was also adapted by Horace for his purposes. He variously addresses Apollo, Diana, Venus, Mercury, the Muses Clio, Calliope and Melpomene, Fortune, Bacchus and Faunus, often only to move into an unlocalized scene or sentiment which may be lightly felt or deeply serious. He calls on objects which range from the lyre of Alcaeus, dedicated to Apollo (I.32), and the ship (I.14) which is symbolic of the ship of State (an image taken from Alcaeus), and perhaps reflects the political uncertainty which was not wholly removed by the victory of Actium, down to a wine-jar to be broached (III.21) and the notorious tree of II.13 which fell and narrowly missed him. Persons named may be little more than pegs on which to hang great poems – who cares now for Postumus as the poem develops, though his name is reiterated in the first line of II.14?

> Earth, home and kindly wife
> must be left, nor will any of the trees
> you foster, except the unloved cypress,
> follow their brief master.

So too with Sallustius Crispus (II.2), Iccius (I.29), Sestius when 'Sharp winter thaws for the spring and West-Wind' in I.4, and Dellius in II.3, since:

> All are thus compelled;
> early or late the urn is shaken;
> fate will out; a little boat
> shall take us to eternal exile.

As for the girls who flit through the poems, rarely repeated and barely differentiated – Chloe, Galatea, Glycera, Lalage, Lyce, Lyde, Lydia, Myrtale, Pyrrha and Tyndaris, to name a selection – if these are Horace's loves, his attitude towards them would usually seem to involve nothing more profound or disturbing than a gently teasing affection. These docile, often silly young things are treated tenderly but never over-sentimentally, much as the innocent sacrificial victims of whom Horace writes with a kind of sympathy – the young boar 'practising sidelong thrusts' in III.22, the white-marked calf in IV.2, and the touching young kid of III.13:

> a little goat
> whose forehead bumpy with budding
>
> horns prognosticates love and war –
> in vain: the kidling of wanton herds
> shall dye with his scarlet blood
> your icy streams.

Yet Horace can so quickly sheer away into irony and self-parody that it is hard to be sure. Pyrrha, in that much-translated ode I.5, appears to some to have had a real hold on Horace's affections, so that his relief at his escape is genuine; others find the charm of this fine-wrought little poem to lie in its detachment and irony. It is one of the paradoxes of Horace that this most elusive of poets gives rise to a conflict of opinions which are so definitely and personally held. But Lyce in III.10 (who may or may not be the 'agèd crow' of IV.13) is certainly no docile victim, and Horace speaks here in a voice helpless with male frustration. The 'I' who 'will not always tolerate sky, and rain, and doorstep' is not to be taken as Horace himself, but the feeling of powerless subjection throughout the poem is real enough.

The only woman of whom Horace writes differently here (Cinara is not mentioned yet) is the 'lady Licymnia' of II.12. The name is a pseudonym (Horace never names a Roman lady and *domina* implies a wife); the scholiast Porphyrio says that she was Terentia, wife of Maecenas and half-sister to the consul Terentius Varro Murena. For her Horace writes one of his best poems, one of great delicacy and respect. And of course he has his real friends, men of whom or to whom he writes with warm affection: Maecenas, 'the half of my heart', to whom he swore in II.17:

> I have taken
> no false oath: we shall go, we shall go,
> whenever you lead the way, comrades prepared
> to take the last journey together.

The poet Virgil too, in I.3, is 'the half of my soul'; Pompeius is his 'friend and oldest comrade' at Philippi; the poet Quintilius Varus, contemporaries such as Aelius Lamia (I.36) and the unknown Valgius of II.9, are all treated as personal friends.

Horace describes himself as an Epicurean in the much-quoted lines which end *Epistles* I.4:

> Come and see me when you want a laugh. I'm fat and sleek,
> in prime condition, a porker from Epicurus' herd.

His early scepticism, not unlike that of Lucretius, is shown in his amusement at a temple miracle on the famous journey to Brundisium in *Satires* I.5.100–104:

> Apella the Jew
> may believe it – not me, for I have learned that the gods live a life
> of calm, and that if nature performs a miracle, it's not
> sent down by the gods in anger from their high home in the sky.

The philosophy would suit his need for detachment and enjoyment of the simple pleasures of the day, though he shows no deeper interest in Epicurean teaching; and he combines his scepticism with an apparent acceptance of the Olympian gods as great poetic figures, and with an affection for unsophisticated ritual in a country setting, comparable with an unbeliever's pleasure in the Christmas story or evensong in a village church.[7] So at the Faunalia in III.18:

> The whole flock plays on the grassy plain
> when the Nones of December come round;
> in the fields the parish and its idle cattle
>     make their holiday;
>
> the wolf now roams among fearless lambs;
> for you the wild-wood sheds its leaves;
> and the ditch-digger loves to tread his opponent
>     earth in three-four time.

As always, his irony makes it difficult to know when he is serious. I.34 ('A parsimonious and infrequent worshipper') can hardly be taken' as a conversion, and quickly passes on to the capriciousness of Fortune. But in areas where he is totally committed there is no understatement, no teasing vanishing trick, no

7. Wilkinson, p.28.

*persona* lightly assumed and tossed aside. He is very conscious of his vocation as a poet, and has a real sense of being under divine protection. The Bacchic and Dionysian odes on the poet's inspiration show genuine ecstasy (II. 19, II. 20 and, as follows, III. 25):

> O master of the Naiads
> and Bacchanalians strong to uproot the princely ash,
>
> I shall utter nothing
> insignificant, lowly or not immortal. Sweet the risk,
> Lenaean, to follow the God,
> crowning one's brows with sprouting vine leaves.

Poems which celebrate the liberating influence of god-given wine are also written with sure simplicity; in III. 21:

> you bring back hope to despairing minds;
> add spirit and strength to the poor,
> who after you tremble neither at the crowns
> of angry kings nor at the soldiery's weapons.

Often his need to disengage himself from what he sees as corruptive influences on mankind, and his enjoyment of immediate pleasures are set against his acute awareness of life's uncertainties and of the inexorable advance of death which is the end of all; thus II. 18:

> What more can you need? Earth
>
> opens impartially for paupers
> and the sons of kings, and Charon could not
> be bribed to ferry back
> even resourceful Prometheus. He holds
>
> Tantalus and Tantalus'
> progeny, and whether or not invoked
> is alert to disburden
> the serf when his labour is done.

Horace was not by temperament melancholic, in the way Virgil was; but his sense of *lacrimae rerum* is no less poignant and profound because it is so simply, even baldly expressed by one who chose on the whole to smile – if wryly – at himself and the vanities of life. Any suggestion that because Horace was never openly anguished or resentful he was no more than a tubby little man fond of girls and good wine fails to see that no less than Marvell he felt at his own back Time's wingèd chariot hurrying near; and that he well understood how the poet's heightened awareness gives him the power – even the duty – to speak for the civilized values as he understands them.

Of course Horace was a Roman of his time, and as such accepted uncritically certain things which we find hard to take today: animal sacrifice, for instance, and the institution of slavery to provide him with girls for his entertainment, and labourers and managers for his farm. Still less could he escape the troubled period in which he lived; the Sabine farm was no ivory tower. Horace's most impressionable years had been lived during the tension and violence which followed the murder of Caesar, and that wise father of the Satires must also have remembered the earlier civil wars ending in the death of Pompey. The Epodes were markedly affected by the continuing insecurity after Actium, and several of the Odes – I.2, I.12 (prompted by the dynastic marriage of the young Marcellus and Augustus' daughter Julia) and I.14, with its sense of foreboding – arise out of the fear that after his victory Octavian (Augustus) would last no longer than his predecessors. In spite of Augustus' successes in Spain and Illyria, there is uncertainty on the frontiers – Tiridates in Parthia in I.26 – and anxiety for Augustus in I.35:

> Preserve our Caesar, soon to go out
> against ultimate Britain; preserve our young
> recruits, soon to plant fear in Eastern
> realms and along the Arabian seaboard.

The horrors of civil war, the theme of II.1, addressed to the historian Asinius Pollio, recur; and the repeated allusions to the evils of the getting and spending which wasted Rome's powers, along with the nostalgia for a happier society, all stem from Horace's longing for security.

In 28 B.C. Augustus embarked on a series of social reforms, mainly concerned with marriage and education, and in 27 he 'restored the Republic', claiming for his own authority no more than a tribune's powers as representative of the people. This is what is called the Augustan revival, for which Livy, Virgil and Horace were spokesmen; though Horace, as a native of a Hellenized south Italy, was perhaps never so wholehearted a 'Roman' as the others. It is easy now to be critical of one-man rule in the interests of efficiency and the domestic virtues; many of us have seen what price could be paid for making the trains run on time and supporting a doctrine of *Kinder, Küche und Kirche*. Tacitus, writing over a century later, bitterly condemned the Augustan revolution for its destruction of liberty:

> He seduced the army with bonuses, and his cheap food policy was a successful bait for civilians. Indeed, he attracted everybody's goodwill by the enjoyable gift of peace. Then he gradually pushed ahead and absorbed the functions of the senate, the officials, and even the law. Opposition did not exist. War or judicial murder had disposed of all men of spirit. Upper-class survivors found that slavish obedience was the way to succeed, both politically and financially. They had profited from the revolution, and so now they liked the security of the existing arrangement better than the dangerous uncertainties of the old regime.[8]

Horace was probably not very politically enthusiastic. For the Epicurean the dignity of office, which Augustus was always trying to persuade his senators to assume (and which Maecenas consistently refused) was less important than the banishment of care; but a quiet simple life could be comfortably led only against a stable background. There are few specific references to Augustan reforms. III.6 appears to refer to Augustus' programme to rebuild the temples in the hopes of checking the moral degeneracy of which Horace was always conscious, but the beauty of the poem lies in its backward glance:

> . . . manly comrades, yeoman soldiers
> taught to turn the soil with Sabine hoes
> and carry cut firewood at a strict
> mother's bidding when the Sun
>
> advanced the shadows of the hills
> and lifted the yokes from weary steers,
> his departing chariot leading in
> the hours of comfort.

8. *Annals*, I.2, translated by Michael Grant.

And the link with Regulus as a symbol of Rome's heroic past, much as Livy saw it, is what gives III. 5 its visionary breadth. It is customary to group as 'political odes', all written in the somewhat solemn Alcaic metre, the first six odes of Book III. These noble poems form Horace's main tribute to the new regime, inspired by the cautious hope that in the emperor's hands Rome would take a new turn. It is noticeable that he is not carried away – he never allows himself to call Augustus a god, only to *associate* him with the gods – but his sincerity in these grander, Pindaric measures is not to be doubted, even if he has won more affection through his personal lyrics.

When the Odes appeared in 23 B.C. they were poorly received. The depth of Horace's disappointment may be measured by the fact that he gave up writing lyrics for some six years and reverted to the smooth-flowing hexameters of the Satires in his conversational verse letters. A first book of these Epistles was brought out in 20–19 B.C. Horace addresses Maecenas in the first of the twenty poems (*Epistles* I. 1. 10–15):

> So now I'm laying aside my verses and other amusements.
> My sole concern is the question 'What is right and proper?'
> I'm carefully storing things for use in the days ahead.
> In case you wonder whom I follow and where I'm residing,
> I don't feel bound to swear obedience to any master.
> Where the storm drives me I put ashore and look for shelter.

So his intention was to withdraw from the urban rat-race and seek contentment in his ideal country life.

Three more long epistles (which include the *Art of Poetry*) provided a second book and appeared, it is generally thought, soon after 17 B.C. In the first, addressed to Augustus at his request, Horace defends the role of the poet and modern poetry against the prejudices of the Roman public in favour of archaic Latin verse, however unintelligible.

> If poems like wine improve with age, would somebody tell me
> how old a page has to be before it acquires value?
> Take a writer who sank to his grave a century back –
> where should he be assigned? To the unapproachable classics
> or the worthless moderns?

Suppose the Greeks had resented newness as much as we do,
what would now be old? And what would the people have
to read and thumb with enjoyment, each man to his taste?

*(Epistles* II.1.34–8, 90–93)

The second is a wry apology for his abandoning lyric poetry:

And yet it's best to be sensible – to throw away one's toys
and leave to children the sort of games that suit their age,
and instead of hunting for words to set to the lyre's music
to practise setting one's life to the tunes and rhythms of truth.

*(Epistles* II.2.141–4)

In the *Ars Poetica* (303–5) he justifies his shift to literary criticism:

No one could put together better poems; but really
it isn't worth it. And so I'll play the part of a grindstone
which sharpens steel but has no part itself in the cutting.

But the tone of *Epistles* I.19, addressed to Maecenas, who *did*
appreciate the extent of Horace's achievement, is unusually bitter
(35–41):

Perhaps you would like to know why readers enjoy and praise
my pieces at home, and ungratefully run them down in public?
I'm not the kind to hunt for the votes of the fickle rabble
by standing dinners and giving presents of worn-out clothes.
I listen to distinguished writers and pay them back; but I don't
approach academic critics on their platforms to beg their support.
Hence the grief.

Yet it is understandable that the Odes were caviare to the
general. Not only were they difficult metrically, but the purists
could and did criticize them for the Latin innovations Horace
introduced into the Greek lyric metres. The language is highly
compressed, the allusions often cryptic, the mythology sometimes
obscure. *Odes* III.3 ('The just man tenacious of his purpose') is a
noble poem of reconciliation expressed mainly through Juno's
speech, which is hard at first to grasp unless it is remembered that
she had supported the Trojans in the Trojan War, and that Romu-
lus was her descendant and founder of the new city of which
Augustus was the second founder. To understand why Teucer is

introduced into *Odes* I.7 we have to know that after Teucer returned from the Trojan War without his brother Ajax, he was sent straight into exile by his father Telamon, and that Horace's friend the consul Plancus had permitted or procured the proscription of *his* brother in 42 B.C., many years before this poem was written; cf. Velleius Paterculus II.67.3–4, quoted by West, p.115, and the notes to this poem, p.205. So if Teucer could find comfort in wine, Plancus can too.

Such detail delights commentators, but does it make for immediate appreciation of a poem? Horace is careful to contrive an appearance of casualness in the shifts of tone in his long poems, as he does in his ordering of serious and lighter poems in each book, and each ode is entirely self-contained, with nothing like a title or any opening lines to set a scene. All this can create difficulty, and outside the sophisticated coterie surrounding Maecenas a Roman audience may well have found it a puzzling collection. Being so far removed in time, we are likely to find it even more puzzling, though possibly less daunting, accustomed as we are to grappling with obscurities and allusions and metrical inventions in the poetry of Hopkins, Yeats and Eliot, and to turning to factual notes (such as are provided for this translation) to resolve the initial problems. We no longer look for a 'message' of the kind we expect from Virgil or Wordsworth, and the sudden surprises of the Odes may be more in keeping with our own fragmented moods in an uncertain age.

If Horace's contemporaries were irritated by his elusiveness and felt that they could never pin him down, it might also be because in the two books of Satires he had already established a more consistent self-portrait as an altogether more genial figure – *l'homme moyen sensuel* who took a humorous view of himself and of life's oddities; and, in *Epistles* I.20.24–5, he was to describe himself as

Of small build, prematurely grey, and fond of the sun,
    he was quick to lose his temper, but not hard to appease.

But the Horace of the Odes wears so many masks: amused and ironic in one poem, he castigates moral corruption in the next; the heart-aching beauty of the spring's renewal becomes a *memento mori* under the inexorable advance of 'Pallid Death'; the proud awareness of the poet's calling slides into the disclaimer (I.6):

> Flippant as ever, whether afire
> or fancy free, I sing of banquets and 'battles'
> of eager girls with neatly trimmed nails
> against the young men.

Life for Horace at this time was generally less kind. Twice he mentions his poor health (*Epistles* I.7 and 15), and there had been reminders of mortality. The poet Quintilius Varus died in 24; Virgil and Tibullus in 19 B.C. The charmed circle round Maecenas suffered in late 23 when the leakage of the discovery of conspiracy against the emperor was traced to Maecenas, who had mentioned it to his wife, half-sister of a conspirator.[9] After this Maecenas ceased to be of influence with Augustus, though Horace himself seems to have been on increasingly friendly terms – to the extent of being a butt for Augustus' heavy, somewhat schoolboyish humour.[10]

It was in fact Augustus who brought Horace back to writing lyric poetry by commissioning the Centennial Hymn (*carmen saeculare*) to commemorate the revival of the Secular Games in 17 B.C. This was to be a typical Horatian ode, written in Sapphics, sung by a double choir of boys and girls, addressed to Apollo and Diana,

> not meant to be part of the religious ceremonies but to be an ideal image of them, and therefore to be performed after the completion of all the sacrifices. By making this arrangement Augustus and his advisers showed that they respected the limits which Horace himself had set to his art. They encouraged him to persist in his own manner because they understood the meaning and aims of his poetry. This complete recognition stirred Horace profoundly. Disappointment and resignation gave way to fresh impulses, and the damned-up stream of his lyrics began to flow again.[11]

The Centennial Hymn is a triumphal ode which is unique in the way it breathes serenity. The prayers it offers are a list of the Augustan regime's achievements in establishing peace, security and prosperity:

9. Suetonius, *The Twelve Caesars*: Augustus 66.3.
10. See Appendix, p.195.
11. Fraenkel, p. 382.

Now the Parthian fears the Alban axes,
the forces mighty by sea and land;
now Scythians and Indians, lately so proud,
      await our answer.

Now Faith, and Peace, and Honour,
and pristine Modesty, and Manhood neglected,
dare to return, and blessèd Plenty appears
      with her laden horn.

Its reception put Horace somewhat in the position of poet laureate.
Thus he had good reason to ask in *Epistles* II.1.132–3:

Where would innocent boys and girls who are still unmarried
have learnt their prayers if the Muse had not vouchsafed them a
      poet?

Augustus then asked him to follow up this highly professional
poem with odes to commemorate the victories of his stepsons
Tiberius and Drusus over the Alpine tribes, and to add a fourth to
his three books of Odes.

   There are fifteen poems in the final collection, generally thought
to have been brought out in 13 B.C. or rather later, about ten years
after the earlier lyrics. The two victory odes requested are 4 and 14;
2 is also in the grand style – it is Horace's tactful refusal to write a
Pindaric ode to celebrate the triumphal return of Augustus from
Gaul in 16 B.C., and is his final tribute to 'the swan of Dirce' by
contrast with his own 'small talent' expressed in lines 27–32:

      . . . but I, very much in the manner
            of a Matine bee

      laboriously harvesting thyme
      from numerous groves and the banks of many-
      streamed Tibur, inconspicuously accrete
            my intricate verses.

Odes 5 and 15 directly address Augustus: 5 appears to have been
composed during his absence in Gaul and Spain in 13 B.C., while 15
is an epilogue to sum up his country's debt to the emperor. Both
express Horace's hopes for continued peace and security – to be
celebrated, as ever, by festive wine-drinking in a rural scene. The

earlier vision of the poet's calling has now grown (in odes 8 and 9)
into a splendid assurance of immortality for Horace's own lyrics
and for their subjects, since 'The Muse forbids the praiseworthy
man to die./The Muse bestows heaven . . .' (IV.8.28 –9) and

> Many heroes lived before Agamemnon,
> but all are oppressed in unending night,
> unwept, unknown, because they lack
> a dedicated poet.
>
> (IV.9.25–8)

Now that Horace is more Augustus' man and his *persona* is a public
one, many of us will agree with Wilkinson (p.86) that there is some
'blunting of sensibility. The poet who had shown such fine
imaginative sympathy for the captive barbarian boy and girl in the
ode *Icci beatis* (I.29) now mentions the courage of the Rhaetians
fighting in defence of their freedom merely as enhancing the
prowess of the young Tiberius':

> a fine sight in martial combat
> for the chaos he made in havocking
> those resolved to die unconquered . . .
>
> (IV.14.17–19)

But we have not lost the Horace we knew. The seventh ode looks
back to the fourth in the first book, written in similar (Archi-
lochian) metre and on the same theme – the return of spring and the
reminder in the recurring seasons that for man there is no return –
and A. E. Housman was not alone in thinking this Horace's most
beautiful poem. Spring when 'meadows no longer are frozen, nor
do/the rivers roar, turgid with winter's snow' (IV.12)[12] also
prompts the invitation to Vergilius to

> Set aside delay and thought of gain
> and mindful of darkness burning mix
> brief sottishness with wisdom while you may:
> it is sweet to play the clown upon occasion.

12. See further K. Quinn in *Latin Explorations*, Chapter 1: 'Horace's Spring Odes'
(IV.12,I.4, IV.7).

And if Phyllis, invited in IV.11 to celebrate Maecenas' birthday in simple domestic revels, is the 'last of my loves' and recalls all the Greek-named girls who have gone before, the opening poem, in which the middle-aged poet calls on Venus for mercy now that desire has awakened in him 'after so long a truce', is one of Horace's most poignant – not for the Ligurinus who is the cause of the awakening (the boy of the lightweight IV.10), but for the bleak statement:

> I am not as I was in the reign
> of my dear Cinara . . .

Cinara is mentioned twice in the Epistles, each time with regret for departed youth. In *Epistles* I.7.25–8

> . . . you'll have to restore
> the strong lungs and the black hair thick on my forehead,
> the charm of words, the well-mannered laughter, and the sad laments
> uttered, with glass in hand, when naughty Cinara left me.

*Epistles* I.14.32–5 is in the same strain:

> the man who went in for fine togas and sleek hair,
> who charmed, as you know, the greedy Cinara without a present,
> and would drink the clear Falernian wine from midday on,
> is content with a simple meal and a doze on the grass by the river.

So she was *rapax* – greedy for gifts, though she was willing to take Horace empty-handed; she was *proterva* – mischievous, naughty; she left him – and she died young. In *Odes* IV.13 we are told that she had a happy successor – Lyce, now old and wrinkled in answer to Horace's prayer:

> To Cinara
> the Fates allowed few years,
> but Lyce shall be long
>
> preserved, an agèd crow,
> that burning young men may study
> (not without much laughter)
> the torch collapsed in ashes.

This is a cruel poem, but its cruelty is not the cold-blooded, gloating artifice of Epodes 8 and 12; it barely conceals the poet's pain. Cinara's is one name which suggests that Horace's emotions were not limited to the close friendships he cultivated with men, and that there could be an exception to his general attitude to the young women of his poems – kindly, amused and playful, rather than seriously involved.

There is no word from Horace after this, though he lived for some five years. The Suetonian *Life* says only that Maecenas died in 8 B.C., asking Augustus to remember Horace 'as you will myself', and that shortly afterwards, on 27 November in the same year, Horace died at the age of not quite fifty-seven. He was too frail to sign a will but indicated Augustus as his heir, and was buried next to Maecenas on the Esquiline Hill.

About a hundred years later Quintilian published his *Institutio Oratoria*, Book X of which is his famous survey of Greek and Roman literature. What he wrote about Horace's lyric poetry shows that the poet's confidence in his lasting fame had not been misplaced.

> Horace is almost the only one of our lyric poets who is worth reading: for sometimes he rises to great heights; he is full of grace and charm; and he shows variety in his figures of speech and an audacity in his choice of words which is very happily successful.[13]

Juvenal writing at much the same time confirmed that Horace also enjoyed the doubtful honour of being a school textbook:

. . . all those guttering lanterns – one to each pupil
so that every Virgil and Horace is grimed with lampblack
from cover to cover.[14]

This was the future Horace had predicted in *Epistles* I.20 for his little book so eager to be off into the world, and it was repeated in the schools set up by Charlemagne. Through the Middle Ages texts were copied and recopied in the Benedictine monasteries, and from the Renaissance onwards Horace was an important humanist influence on Western Europe, with his special admirers in Petrarch,

---

13 Quintilian, X.1.96.
14. Juvenal, *Sátires* VII.266–7, translated by Peter Green; cf. Quintilian I.8.6.

Marvell, Herrick and Collins, and his philosophy of life (understandably unpopular with the Church) was perhaps best appreciated in the 'enlightened' eighteenth century.[15] Some of his Odes have been translated more than any other classical poems; possibly the changing moods of these short lyrics have been an invitation to poets and scholars to try to capture the essence of what has a special appeal for them. One thinks at once of A. E. Housman's translation of Odes IV.7 (*Diffugere nives*), the intimations of mortality which return with the spring,[16] or of Milton's 'What slender youth bedew'd with liquid odours' (his version of I.5, 'Rendered almost word for word without Rhyme according to the Latin Measure, as near as the language will permit'). Translations of this particular ode were assembled by Sir Ronald Storrs and published in 195c under the title *Ad Pyrrham*. They are a selection from the 45 versions which he had collected in twenty-six languages. And u to 1936 there had been over a hundred translations into English o. the complete Odes.[17] Among their authors there have been names justly admired for their achievement in their day: Philip Francis (1743), Christopher Smart (1756), John Conington (1863), Lord Lytton (1869), Sir Edward Marsh (1941).

W. G. Shepherd is therefore conscious that he comes at the end of a long line and takes on the responsibility of presenting Horace for our times. It may seem that his responsibility is the greater because most of his readers will be less steeped in Horace's Latin than their predecessors, whose education was more severely classical. I see this as his advantage: they will not have been worn down, as Byron was at Harrow, by the sheer difficulty of construing the *curiosa felicitas*.

> Then farewell, Horace; whom I hated so,
> Not for thy faults, but mine; it is a curse
> To understand, not feel thy lyric flow,
> To comprehend, but never love thy verse:

15. See further Wilkinson, pp. 159 ff.; Gilbert Highet, *The Classical Tradition*, pp. 124–5, 244–50; and R. M. Ogilvie in *Latin and Greek*, Chapter 2: 'Horace and the Eighteenth Century'.

16. Translations by Sir Thomas Hawkins (1631), Sir Richard Fanshawe (1632), Thomas Creech (1684), and Philip Francis (1743), which Dr Johnson thought the best, compared by Niall Rudd in *Lines of Enquiry*, pp. 189 ff.

17. E. Stemplinger, quoted by Wilkinson, p. 172.

> Although no deeper Moralist rehearse
> Our little life, nor Bard prescribe his art,
> Nor living Satirist the conscience pierce,
> Awakening without wounding the touch'd heart,
> Yet fare thee well – upon Soracte's ridge we part.
> > *Childe Harold's Pilgrimage*, Canto IV, lxxvii

This is a sad admission from one who in maturity showed much of Horace's sanity and urbanity and his freedom from cant and self-deception. But any honest lover of Horace will admit to having had to struggle with his Latin at some time, while others, like Byron, have never really loved his lyric poetry enough to return to it, simply because the initial effort required of them to read it in all the elaboration of an inflected language has seemed too great.

> . . . I wish to express that we become tired of the task before we can comprehend the beauty; that we learn by rote before we can get by heart; that the freshness is worn away, and the future pleasure and advantage deadened and destroyed, by the didactic anticipation, at an age when we can neither feel nor understand the power of compositions which it requires an acquaintance with life, as well as Latin and Greek, to relish, or to reason upon . . .[18]

A fresh translation like this one acts as a kind of liberation, a release into meeting the demands that Horace makes of us as a *poet*.

For the Latinist, reading without prejudice, and with Horace's own words at the back of his mind, there are special delights and surprises: to find, for instance, the pruning metaphor retained in *Odes* I.11, the rare (for Horace) usage of a string of nouns and epithets so neatly presented in the opening lines of III.16, the delicate humour of III.10. W. G. Shepherd's further great advantage is that he is himself a poet, with a poet's perception and gift of words harvested from the marvellous resources of the English language. Through his medium I think we can rediscover Horace and come nearer to understanding his complexity. For myself, I

---

18. From Byron's Note 40 to Stanza lxxv.

have been reading Horace for three quarters of a longish life, never exhausting what he has to offer, and shall continue to read him; and I have been given more than I dared to hope for in this new translation.

BETTY RADICE
*Highgate, 1981*

# SELECT
# BIBLIOGRAPHY

## Texts and Editions

C. E. Bennet, *Horace: Odes and Epodes* (Loeb text and transla-
tion), Cambridge, Mass., and London, 1924

R. G. M. Nisbet and Margaret Hubbard, *A Commentary on Horace:
Odes. Book I*, Oxford, 1970; *Book II*, Oxford, 1978

T. E. Page, *The Odes of Horace*, London, 1883

J. C. Rolfe, *Suetonius: Lives of the Poets* (Loeb), Cambridge, Mass.,
and London, 1970

E. C. Wickham, *Q. Horati Flacci Opera*, revised H. W. Garrod
(O.C.T.), Oxford, 1912

E. C. Wickham, *The Works of Horace: Vol. I. The Odes, Carmen
Saeculare and Epodes*, Oxford, 1877

Gordon Williams, *The Third Book of Horace's Odes*, Oxford, 1969

## Books on Horace

Steele Commager, *The Odes of Horace*, Yale, Newhaven, 1962

C. D. N. Costa, ed., *Horace*, London, 1973

Eduard Fraenkel, *Horace*, Oxford, 1957

Gilbert Highet, *The Classical Tradition*, Oxford, 1949

Gilbert Highet, *Poets in a Landscape*, London, 1957

Giuseppe Lugli, *La Villa d'Orazio nella valle del Licenza*, Rome, 1930

R. M. Ogilvie, *Latin and Greek*, London, 1964

Kenneth Quinn, *Latin Explorations*, London, 1963

Niall Rudd, *Horace: Satires and Epistles* (with *Persius: Satires*), Harmondsworth, 1973, 1979

Niall Rudd, *Lines of Enquiry*, Cambridge, 1976

W. Y. Sellar, *The Roman Poets of the Augustan Age: Horace and the Elegiac Poets*, Oxford, 2nd edn. 1899

Ronald Storrs, *Ad Pyrrham*, Oxford, 1959

J. P. Sullivan, ed., *Critical Essays in Roman Literature: Elegy and Lyric*, London, 1962

David West, *Reading Horace*, Edinburgh, 1967

L. P. Wilkinson, *Horace and his Lyric Poetry*, Cambridge, 1945, 1968

Gordon Williams, *Horace* (New Surveys in the Classics No.6), Oxford, 1972

Gordon Williams, *Tradition and Originality in Roman Poetry*, Oxford, 1968

A. J. Woodman and David West, *Quality and Pleasure in Latin Poetry*, Cambridge, 1975

# TRANSLATOR'S
# FOREWORD

An essential part of the celebrated 'lapidary' quality of Horace's style in the Odes is the perfected craftsmanship with which the Latin vocabulary, grammar and syntax are fitted into complex metres adopted or adapted from Greek lyric poetry. Classical metres are of course quantitative, and as such cannot, according to my ear, be employed in English verse: long and short resolve themselves into stressed and unstressed syllables, and the resultant pattern has a narcotic or humorous effect, or else is merely chaotic.

An obvious alternative is to represent Horace's metric by the use of regular English (i.e. stress) metres. However, if he follows this course, the translator 'translates', as regards metre, only the element of regularity, since stress (in the context of metre, as opposed to speech rhythm) plays no part in Classical poetics. Nor does rhyme.

My own method has been to sacrifice the residual common denominator of regularity in order to write the sort of verse I am best at. I will not describe this as 'free', since the term implies freedom from formal discipline, and I have done what I can to achieve rhythmic cogency, which involves careful control of the number and placing of stressed and unstressed syllables – indeed, some lines derive their motor impulse from approximation to iambic and/or anapaestic and/or dactylic stress-metres.

The metres of the Epodes are in the main straightforward iambics: accordingly, the rhythms of my translations tend to be cruder than for the Odes.

Since my aim has been to make each English poem live *now*, why the archaisms – the occasional Shakespearean or Miltonic echo, the touches of 'Augustan' diction, etc.? These features 'felt right' throughout the period when I was making these translations (1975 –81), and I still approve them. Why? I cannot say for sure, but I can provide a rationale after the event, which I find plausible – which accords, that is, with my conscious attitudes to the translation of Horace.

I feel at once both very close to and very distant from Horace. The closeness is experienced in terms of the patent aesthetic excellence of his work, and the abundant humanity of the *personae* he assumes (or aspects of himself he reveals) therein. The feeling of distance is maintained by Horace's continual reminders that his world was (human nature excepted) so profoundly different from ours: he lived – this is the essential point – so very long ago. Naïve perception of time merges into an awed awareness of duration; of the perdurable vitality and sophistication of Horace's art; of the fact that as a translator of this poet I have across the centuries so many, and in many cases such illustrious, predecessors. Perhaps the archaisms in these versions register, and seek to remind the reader of, that long perspective.

The poems that follow are translations from the Oxford Classical Texts edition, except that I have preferred the following variant readings. EPODES: 2.25 *ripis* for *rivis*; 5.3 *et* for *aut*, 87 *maga non* for *magnum*; 9.17 *hoc* for *hunc*; 16.15 *quod* for *quid*; 17.81 *exitum* for *exitus*. ODES: I.7.17 *perpetuos* for *perpetuo*; I.8.2 *oro* for *vere*; I.12.41 *intonsis* for *incomptis*; I.15.20 *crines* for *cultus*; I.25.2 *ictibus* for *iactibus*, 20 *Euro* for *Hebro*; I.27.19 *laboras in* for *laborabas*; I.31.9 *Calena* for *Calenam*, 10 *ut* for *et*, 18 *et* for *at*; I.32.15 *medicumque* for *mihi cumque*; I.38.6 *cura* for *curo*; II.13.38 *laborum* for *laborem*; III.3.12 *bibet* for *bibit*, 54 *tangat* for *tanget*; III.4.9 *avio* for *Apulo*, 38 *addidit* for *abdidit*; III.14.11 *non* for *iam;* III.24.4 *publicum* for *Apulicum*; III.26.7 *securesque* for *et arcus*; IV.2.49 *tuque* for *terque*;

IV.4.17 *Raetis* for *Raeti*; IV.9.31 *silebo* for *sileri*; IV.10.5 *Ligurine* for *Ligurinum*.

Working on this project has been an engrossing and profoundly satisfying task: it has also involved me in some of the hardest work I have ever undertaken, so the interest shown by friends and correspondents has helped me greatly. I thank the following people, who have given encouragement and/or criticism and/or have accepted poems for publication or broadcasting: my wife Margaret, Michael Benson, Professor C. O. Brink, William Cookson, Dick Davis, Elsie Durrans, Tony Greaves, Peter Jay, Tom Lowenstein, Donald McFarlan, J. H. Prynne, Michael Schmidt, C. H. Sisson, Fraser Steel, Alison Wade, John Welch and Peter Whigham.

Natural justice requires that I make separate mention of Betty Radice. She provided me with comments covering draft versions of *all* the poems in this book: in many cases her scholarship and acute feeling for language proved extremely helpful. Also, I am most grateful for her assistance with the notes and glossary.

W. G. SHEPHERD
*Southgate, 1981*

# EPODES

# I

## *Ibis Liburnis*

You advance our light Liburnian galleys
'gainst towering bulwarks, friend Maecenas,
prepared yourself to undergo
all Caesar's perils. But what of us
whose life, if you survive,
is joy; if not, a burden?
Shall we pursue a docile ease
not sweet with you away,
or endure your rigours with the hearts
of not unmanly men? We shall                                    10
endure, and over the Alpine peaks
or uninhabitable Caucasus
or far as the farthest bays of the West
shall follow with fortitude. I am not
warlike and I lack resolve, so how,
you ask, can my endeavours aid yours?
Your comrades know the less,
as those away the greater, fear —
the broody bird dreads gliding serpents
most for the featherless chicks                                 20
she has left, though her presence
could bring them no help. This and every
war should be willingly fought
in hope of your approbation —
not that more bullocks may strain
forward yoked to my ploughs;
nor that before the parching
Dog-Days come my herds may change
Calabrian for Lucanian grazing;
nor in hope of a spick and span villa                           30
abutting on lofty Tusculum's Circean walls.
Your favour has enriched me enough

and more: I will not lay up wealth
to bury in the earth like miserly Chremes
or squander like some feckless heir.

## 2

## *Beatus ille*

'Happy he who far from business dealing
(like uncorrupted folk of yore)
and free from interest owing,
works with his oxen his family land:
no soldier he aroused by fierce alarums;
nor does he dread the sea enchaf'd;
he avoids the haughty portals of
great men, and likewise the Forum;
he weds his lofty poplar trees
to nubile shoots of vine;                              10
in some secluded dale reviews
his lowing, wandering herds;
he prunes back barren shoots
with his hook and grafts on fruitful;
he stores pressed honey in clean jars;
he shears the harmless sheep;
when Autumn lifts in the fields his head
fittingly decked with ripened fruit,
he delights to pluck the grafted pears
and grapes that vie with the purple,                   20
with which to render thanks to you,
Priapus, and you, father Silvanus,
the guardian of bound'ries.
Pleasant now to recline beneath a tree,
and now on some luxuriant sward
as the waters glide by lofty banks,
birds quire in the woods
and purling brooklets babble,

lulling to gentle slumber.
But when the winter of thundering Jove     30
brings in rain and snow,
one either harries with hounds
hither and thither fierce boars
into the intercipient toils,
or stretches loose nets on smooth poles
to deceive the eager thrushes,
and takes with a noose the pleasant prize
of coward hare and migrant crane.
Who will recall to remembrance
amid such things the woeful pangs of love?     40
But if a modest helpmeet plays her part
with home and sweet children
(a Sabine dame or sun-tanned wife
of some Apulian stalwart),
and piles the blessèd hearth with seasoned faggots
against the coming of her weary spouse,
and pens the frisking flock with wattle,
and drains their swelling udders,
and pours the sweet new vintage from its jar,
and prepares a repast of home-produce;     50
then Lucrine oysters could not rejoice
me more, nor turbot, nor scar,
when Winter booming on waves of Dawn
diverts them to our fishing-grounds;
neither African fowl nor Ionian pheasant
descends more pleasantly into my belly
than olives picked out from the richest boughs,
or sorrel that thrives in the fields,
or mallows good for bodily ailments,
or a lamb slaughtered at the feast of Terminus,     60
or a kidling saved from the wolf.
Amid such feasts it is a joy to see
the sheep hasting home from pasture,
the wearied oxen dragging along
with languid necks the upturned ploughshares,
the home-bred slaves (the swarm of a thriving house)
about the glittering Lares . . . '

– Thus Alfius, a moneylender,
on the point of turning farmer:
he called in all his capital                                70
on the Ides, and on the Kalends
he's busily loaning it out again.


# 3

## *Parentis olim*

He whose impious hand has strangled
his agèd father deserves to eat it. It is
more harmful than hemlock. Garlic.
Peasants must have iron guts.
What venom rages in my gizzard?
Have these roots been stewed
in vipers' blood without my knowledge?
Has Canidia handled this evil dish?
Medea infatuate with the Argonauts' captain
(more fair than all his crew)                              10
when he tried to yoke the unbroken bulls
anointed her Jason with this;
and before she fled on the great winged worm
she took revenge on his mistress
by making her gifts besmeared with this.
Never did such a fiery, stifling heat
settle on drought-parched Apulia.
Nessus' shirt did not sear
more swelteringly into
resourceful Hercules' shoulders.                           20
If ever you are tempted this way again,
my humorous Maecenas, I devoutly hope
that your girl will push away your face
and retreat to the very edge of the bed.

# 4

## *Lupis et agnis*

As falls by fate between wolves and lambs,
so is the strife 'twixt me and you,
whose flanks are callous'd from Spanish bonds
and shanks from hard shackles.
Although you stroll puffed up with wealth,
Fortune does not change your kind.
Don't you see, as you perambulate
the Sacred Way in your toga of twice three yards,
the faces of passers-by, this side and that,
express the most patent indignation?                    10
– 'This creature, once flogged with the magistrates' lash
till the crier himself was sickened,
now ploughs a thousand acres of good Falernian land.
His ponies wear out the Appian Way.
Defying Otho's law, he takes his place
like an eminent knight in the foremost seats.
What can be gained by sending so many
beaked warships of massive tonnage
against the pirates and bands of slaves
when this, this thing, is an army tribune?'              20

# 5

## *At, o deorum*

'But o whatever Gods in heaven rule
the earth and humankind,
what does this hubbub mean, and what
the fearsome staring of all at me?
By your children (if summoned
Lucina attended honest births),
by this vain favour of purple,

by Jupiter bound to disapprove
these things, I beseech you, why
do you glare like a stepmother,                                    10
or feral animal goaded with steel?'
– Having made this plaint with
trembling lips, stripped of his emblems
the boy stood firm, a childlike form
to soften savage Thracian hearts.
Her unkempt hirsute poll
all tangled with little vipers,
Canidia orders funereal cypress,
wild fig-trees dug out from tombs,
a nocturnal screech-owl's feathers and eggs            20
smeared with the blood of a nasty toad,
herbs supplied by poisonous-
fertile Iolcos and Spain,
bones snatched from a starving bitch –
to be scorched in the Colchian flames.
Sagana, like a sea-urchin
bristling in her shift,
or like some charging boar,
sprinkles water from Lake Avernus
through all the house. Veia,                                    30
phlegmatic because amoral,
groaning over her labour,
digs up the earth with a spade.
And buried there, with only his face
protruding, and only so much
as a person's in water floating
suspended from his chin,
the boy can starve to death
in full view of a dinner
changed twice or thrice in each long day:            40
once his eyes, on the unattainable food,
have withered away, his marrow and liver,
excised and dried, will serve
for an aphrodisiac potion.
And the gossips of Naples and all
the neighbouring towns believe

that the mannish-lustful hag
Arimensian Folia was there,
who by Thessalian incantations
tears moon and stars from the sky.
Then fearsome Canidia, gnawing
her uncut nails with her bile-black teeth,
what did she say, what leave unsaid?
'O faithful witnesses of these my deeds,
Night, and Diana who rules in the silence
when holy myst'ries are performed,
now come, now come, now turn your wrath
and godhead-power on hostile homes.
While weary predators sweetly slumb'ring
lie hid in the dreadful forest, let
the Subura's curs all yap at the ancient rake
smeared with a lotion as perfect
as any my hands have contrived.
What's wrong? Why don't the terrible drugs
of outlandish Medea prevail
with which before she fled she took revenge
on the haughty concubine,
the daughter of mighty Creon,
when the given mantle steeped in pus
took off with burning the newlywed bride?
No roots or herbs in hiding
in overgrown nooks escaped me:
he slumbered on perfumed bedding,
oblivious to all female charms.
But oh! Oh! He walks, set free
by the spell of some more learnèd witch.
By no familiar draught, my Varus,
o creature bound for bitter grieving,
shall you come running back to me,
and by no Marsian incantation shall
your understanding be restored.
I shall brew a stronger, pour a yet stronger
draught to physic your revulsion,
and sooner shall the sky sink down
beneath the sea, the earth spread out above,

50

60

70

80

than you not blaze with love for me
like smoking pitch in fire.'
– At this the boy no longer, as before,
would calm the unnatural hags
with soothing words, ·                                    90
but doubtful how to break his silence
flung out Thyestean curses.
'Your poison-magic has no power
to alter right and wrong
or turn aside human retribution.
My curses shall dog you:
no sacrifice may avert
my solemn execrations.
And when, my death enjoined,
I have breathed my last, I shall                         100
waylay you by night as a Fury; my shade
shall slash at your faces with crookèd nails,
as Manes are empowered to do;
and squatting upon your unquiet breasts,
I shall keep off sleep with terror.
The rabble, this side and that,
shall pulp you, you senile
obscenities, by pelting you with rocks.
Then the Esquiline wolves and carrion birds
shall scatter your unburied limbs:                       110
this spectacle shall not escape
my parents, outliving me, alas.'


# 6

## *Quid immerentis hospites*

A cowardly cur when facing wolves,
why do you harass innocuous strangers?
You do not dare to turn your empty threats
this way? Bait me, who will bite you back?

Molossian hound or tawny Laconian,
the shepherd's strong right arm,
ears pricked, I'll follow amid deep snow
whatever predator leads on.
Having filled the woods with threat'ning yelps,
you sniff at the meat that's flung you.                          10
Take care, take care: I ferociously lift
my ready horns against rank malice,
like the slighted son-in-law of Lycambes
the false, or Bupalus' eager opponent.
Worried with poisonous teeth,
should I blub like a child, unavenged?

# 7

## Quo, quo, scelesti ruitis?

Into what, what, do you wickedly plunge?
Why do your hands draw swords from scabbards?
Perhaps too little Latin blood has been spilled
on battlefields or Neptune's realm?
And not that Romans might burn
the haughty towers of emulous Carthage;
not that the scatheless Briton might trudge
in chains down the Sacred Way;
but that in fulfilment of Parthian prayers
this City might die by her own right hand.                       10
Such 'haviour never 'longed to lions or wolves,
ferocious only to alien kinds.
Does blinded frenzy possess us?
Some sharper goad, such as guilt? Reply!
– Silence. A blenching pallor dyes their cheeks,
their capsized intellects are numb.
So it goes: a bitter fate pursues
the Romans, and the crime of fratricide,
since the blood of Remus ran on the earth,
the bane of his successors.                                      20

# 8

## *Rogare longo*

That you, rotten, should ask what it is
that emasculates me, when you've
just one black tooth and decrepit age
ploughs up your forehead with wrinkles,
when a diarrhoeic cow's hole gapes
between your dehydrated buttocks!
What rouses me is your putrid bosom,
your breasts like the teats of a mare,
the flaccid belly and skinny thighs
that top your grossly swollen shanks.   10
Be bless'd, and may triumphant lovers'
likenesses attend your corpse.
May no wife perlustrate laden
with fatter, rounder pearls than yours.
What though Stoic pamphlets like
to lie between silken pillows?
Illiterate sinews stiffen,
and hamptons droop, no less for that.
(Though if you hope to rouse up mine,
your mouth is faced with no mean task.)   20

# 9

## *Quando repostum Caecubum*

My bless'd Maecenas, when shall you and I,
in your lofty palace, rejoicing in
Caesar's triumph, as is grateful to Jove,
drink the Caecuban put up for special feasts,
while the lyre propounds the Dorian mode
in consort with exotic pipes? – As when,
of late, Neptune's admiral Pompey,

his ships all burned, was driven from the sea
and fled, though he had threatened the City
with fetters struck off from the treacherous slaves    10
his friends. – Alas when Romans, bought and sold
(posterity will deny it), bear stakes
and weapons for a woman; when soldiers
can bring themselves to serve under withered
eunuchs; and among the Army's standards
the sunshine brights a shameful pavilion –
at which two thousand Gauls, chanting the name
of Caesar, swerved aside their snorting mounts;
and rebel warships signalled to the left
lay hid in harbour. Hail Triumph! You'd not    20
keep back the victor's chariots of gold,
the unyoked kine? Hail Triumph! You brought us
no such general back from Jugurtha's war –
not Africanus, whose manhood built his tomb
upon Carthage. Defeated on land and sea,
the foe has changed his crimson cloak for mourning;
and is either sailing mazed among cross winds
to Crete and her hundred storied cities;
or makes for the Syrtes the south wind keeps
in exercise; or is borne away upon    30
uncharted seas. Boy! bring larger goblets
and Chian or Lesbian wine, or measure out
Caecuban to settle our seasick stomachs:
it is sweet to disperse with Bacchus' aid
our anxious concern for Caesar's affairs.

# 10

## *Mala soluta navis*

The ship sets her sail and leaves,
rank-smelling Maevius on board.
Auster, do not omit to lash
her port and starb'd with waves.

Scatter her rigging and splintered oars,
Eurus, on somersaulting seas.
Arise, Aquilo, as though to rend
the thrumming oaks of the mountain heights.
May no kind star appear
in the lowering night when harsh Orion sets.          10
Let him be borne upon no calmer sea
than was the band of victorious Greeks
when Pallas turned her rage from Ilium burned
to sacrilegious Ajax' craft.
What sweating lies in wait for your crew –
what muddy pallor for you, unmanly shrieking,
and prayers to inattentive Jove,
when Notus howling across
the Ionian gulf shall smash your keel . . .
And if prime carrion sprawled          20
on the curving shore shall entertain
the gulls, a randy goat and a lamb
shall be killed for the Tempest Gods.


## I I

## *Petti, nihil me*

Pettius, no longer does it delight me as before
to write my verses, for I am stricken with love –
with love, that seeks me out before all others
to ignite my yearning for tender boys and girls.
The third December shakes the glory from the woods
since my infatuate warmth for Inachia ceased.
I was (alas) a weighty theme of city gossip:
I am ashamed of so much slander. The silence
and listlessness at dinner that proved me in love,
and the sighs fetched up from the depths of my lungs,          10
now grieve me. 'A poor man's inherent qualities
have no value when weighed with wealth,' I would complain

to you, in tears, as soon as the injudicious God's
impetuous wine elicited my secret thoughts.
'But if honest resentment should come to the boil
in my breast, and scatter to the winds these ineffective
fomentations (that no way ease my grievous wound),
supplanted propriety shall break off the unequal strife.'
And having sternly met your eyes and praised this course,
told to go home I made my way with faltering steps          20
to a door (alas) inimical (alas) to me
and steps of stone on which I bruised my sides and thighs.
Love of Lyciscus holds me now, who prides himself
that his tenderness surpasses that of any girl,
from whom no frank advice or urgent contumely
on the part of my friends can set me free,
but only another blaze of desire, for a fair girl
or a sleek boy, long hair put up in a knot.


# I 2

## *Quid tibi vis*

'What's up, lady most apt for elephantine niggers?
Why send me presents and letters, although
I am no strapping youth, have no distended nose –
yet I sniff out the polyp or goat that beds
in your armpits' bushes more shrewdly
than does the keenest hound where the boar lies hid.'
– The cock gone slack, what sweat, what evil stench,
envelops all her withered limbs
as she hastes to placate her invincible madness;
foundation cream tinted with crocodile crap,                10
damp powdered chalk, will not adhere; her lust
makes the overtaxed bedding and canopy split.
Or else she mocks my revulsion with these fierce jibes:
'You flag with Inachia less than with me:
you manage Inachia thrice in one night, to me

you are nice and make the effort just once.
An ill death may that Lesbia die who discovered
your impotence when I looked for a bull,
when Amyntas of Cos was mine for the taking,
in whose invincible groin is stuck a member        20
more resolute than a burgeoning mountain tree.
For whom are those woollens hurriedly dyed
again and again in Tyrian purples? For you,
of course, in case in your age-group
there should be found a guest whose mistress values him
more highly than you. Oh! I am so unhappy;
you flee me as lambs fear wolves, as deer fear lions.'

# 13

## *Horrida tempestas*

A violent tempest narrows the heaven, and rain
and snow-storms lead down Jove: now seas, now forests
resound with the Thracian north wind. Friends, let us seize
opportunity day by day, and while our limbs are strong
and it suits, let's wipe responsibility from furrowed brows.
Bring a wine that was trod when Torquatus was consul,
and speak of nothing else: kind Bacchus may ameliorate
our cares and put them to bed. Now it is pleasing to be
besprinkled with Persian nard, for Cyllenean lyres
to soothe away from our breasts all ominous disquiet,        10
as the famous Centaur once sang to his stalwart foster-child:
'Invincible, mortal son of Goddess Thetis,
Assaracus' land awaits you, which the chilly streams
of little Scamander divide, and perilous Simois,
your return from which the Fates' immutable weft
debars – your sea-blue mother may not bring you home:
relieve all evils there with wine and song,
sweet ministration to ugly hurts.'

# 14

## *Mollis inertia*

You crush me, honoured Maecenas, by often asking
why feeble apathy spreads oblivion over
my quintessential faculties, as though
I had sucked with a parched throat
from the cups that bring on Lethean sleep.
The God, the God forbids me
to reach the last verse of the numbers begun,
the lines long promised. They say
that Teian Anacreon, who very often
in simple metres deplored his love                          10
to his hollow tortoise-shell lyre,
burned like this for Samian Bathyllus.
You are singed yourself, poor man.
If your flame is fair as that which ignited
beleaguered Troy, rejoice in your luck.
The promiscuous ex-slave Phryne macerates me.

# 15

## *Nox erat et caelo*

The moon was shining in a cloudless sky
amid the dim stars on the night when you,
your twining arms clinging more tight
than the lofty oak is wound about with ivy,
so soon to mock the mighty Gods' divinity,
swore me an oath that as long as Orion
the sailors' foe should discompose
the wintry sea and the wolf the flock,
as long as the breeze should wave Apollo's

unshorn hair, so long would be our love.                    10
Neaera, my manhood shall grieve you much,
for if Horace contains any man at all
he will not bear being second best
to some swain to whom you give it nightly,
but angrily seek a more suitable girl – nor will
his firmness yield to your errant charms
once fixed resentment has entered in.
– And you, whoever you are, who amble
happy and proud in my misfortune,
though perhaps you are rich in flocks              20
and land and Pactolus flows for you alone
and Pythagoras' reincarnations pose
no problems for you and your beauty
surpasses that of Nireus, alas,
you shall bewail her favours transferred
to another, and I shall laugh last.

# 16

## *Altera iam teritur*

Already another generation
is being ground down by civil war. Rome reels
from her own might. What neighbouring Marsians,
invading bands of Etruscan Porsenna,
Capua's emulous courage, Spartacus'
aspiration, treacherous Allobrox' insurrection,
the German beast with its blue-eyed youth
and Hannibal whom parents wished away
could not destroy or tame, this impious
generation of fated stock will waste              10
and the land belong once more to beasts of prey.
Alas, a heathen conqueror shall spurn our ashes,
his cavalry trample the City with clattering hooves
and wantonly scatter (a sin to behold) Quirinus' bones

that now are shelter'd from wind and sun.
Perhaps you all, or at least the better part,
would try, as behoves you, to shun these heavy wrongs?
Then as the Phocaean people cursed
their fields and ancestral Gods, went into exile
and left their shrines to be the lairs of boars                    20
and rapacious wolves; so let no plan be preferred to that
we go, wherever our feet shall bear us, wherever
the south and boisterous south-west winds shall call us
across the waves. A valid motion? Will any oppose?
Then why delay, since the omens are good, to embark?
But let us swear: — Just as soon as rocks are raised
from the deeps and float, then let it be no sin to return;
no provocation to set our sails for the passage home
when the Po shall wash the Matine peaks,
the Apennine heights jut out in the sea,                           30
wonderful love join monsters in novel passion, tigers
be pleased to mount deer, doves fornicate with hawks,
the trusting herd not fear the tawny lion
and the hairless goat enjoy the briny sea.
Having sworn these oaths and whatever else
has the power to cut off our sweet retreat,
let the whole State go – or the portion better than
the unteachable flock – let the weak and despairing
weigh down their fated beds. But you
who have spirit, cast off womanish grief                           40
and glide away past Etruscan coasts.
Encompassing Ocean awaits us. Let us seek
the rich islands and farms, the blessèd farms,
where every year the earth, untilled, yields corn;
and the vines, unpruned, forever bloom;
and the never failing sprigs of olive bud;
and dusky figs adorn their trees;
and honey drips from the hollow oak; and the stream
with plashing feet leaps lightly down from the lofty crag;
and the goats, unbidden, come to the milking-pail;                 50
and the kindly flock brings home full udders;
and no bear growls around the sheepfold at dusk;
and the soil is never tumescent with snakes.

And, bless'd, we shall wonder at yet more things –
how rainy Eurus does not scour the land
with heavy showers, how the fertile seeds
are not too scorched in the dried-out clods,
since Heaven-Father moderates both extremes.
The pine-built Argo's oarsmen did not venture here,
and no lewd queen of Colchis here set foot;            60
no Sidonian sailors turned their vessels' beaks this way,
nor Ulysses' toiling companions.
No infection harms the cattle,
no planet's sweltering fury blasts the sheep.
Jupiter set apart these shores for a God-fearing race
when he stained with bronze the age of gold:
with bronze, then iron, he hardened the ages, from which,
I prophesy, the godly are offered auspicious escape.


# 17

## *Iam iam efficaci*

'Now at last I salute your potent art,
and kneeling I beg by Proserpina's realm,
by Diana's immovable godhead, by your books
of incantations strong to unfix the stars
and call them down from the sky, Canidia,
leave off at length your supernatural spells
and let the swift wheel reverse, reverse.
Telephus moved to pity Nereus' grandson
'gainst whom in his conceit he had marshalled
the Mysian columns and hurled sharp spears.            10
When the king had left his walls and fallen
(alas) at the feet of stubborn Achilles,
the Trojan women anointed man-slaying Hector
given over to carrion birds and dogs.
By Circe's consent the oarsmen
of toiling Ulysses put off their tough

and bristling hides; then wit and speech
flowed back, and their faces' wonted grace.
Dearly belov'd of sailors and salesmen,
I've paid your fines enough and more.                    20
My youth has fled and modesty's blush
departed; my bones are draped in sallow hide;
my hair is white from your perfumes;
no leisure may intersperse my torment;
night crowds out day, day night, and I cannot ease
my straining lungs by taking breath.
And so I'm forced to believe what I denied:
Sabellian incantations shake the heart,
the head is split by Marsian spells.
What more d'you want? O land and sea, I burn         30
as neither Hercules smeared with Nessus'
black blood nor boiling Aetna's burgeoning flames:
you glow like a manufactory
of Colchian poisons so that, dry ash,
I shall be blown away by injurious winds.
What end or what tax awaits me? Declare it:
I will faithfully pay the punishment enjoined,
prepared to expiate, should you demand
a hundred bullocks, or wish to be sung
to a disingenuous lyre – chaste and honest,              40
a golden constellation, you'll walk among the stars.
Castor incensed at Helen's disrepute,
and Castor's great brother, were won by prayer:
so you (you have the power), deliver me from madness,
o woman unworn by family curses, for you
are no pedantic hag who scatters
nine-day ashes 'mid paupers' graves.
Generous is your heart and pure your hands.
Pactumeius is your issue, yours the blood
that crimsoned the cloths the midwife washed,           50
though you stood up strong after giving birth.'

'Why pour your prayers into ears that are shut?
The rocks that wintry Neptune pounds
with leaping brine are not more deaf to naked sailors.

You divulge the Cotyttian rite, the worship
of liberating Bacchus, and hope to smile unharmed?
High-priest of Esquiline poison-magic,
you fill the City with slander of my good name
and expect to reap no reward? What use
to have enriched Paelignian beldames,                    60
to have mixed ever swifter poisons? The fate
awaiting you is longer drawn out than your prayers:
a wretch, you shall lead a wretched life,
never avoiding yet more distress.
Treacherous Pelops' father, Tantalus,
always in need of the generous banquet, longs for rest;
so longs Prometheus, chained to the eagle;
Sisyphus longs to set his boulder upon
the mountain's peak: but the laws of Jove forbid.
Now you shall yearn to jump from lofty towers,            70
and now to broach your breast with a Noric sword;
sick with loathsome depression, in vain
you shall put the noose about your neck.
I'll mount like a knight your unbroken back,
the world give way before my prodigious ride.
Must I, who can animate waxen dolls
(as your curiosity knows), and tear
the moon from the Pole by my spells,
and raise the ashes of the dead,
and nicely mix aphrodisiac draughts:                     80
must I bewail the period of my art,
shall it not prevail over you?'

# ODES

## BOOK I

# I

## *Maecenas atavis edite*

Maecenas, descended from olden kings,
my rampart and sweet admiration,
some there are whose joy it is to collect
Olympic dust and swerve by the post
with smouldering axle and lift to the Gods
like lords of the earth the winner's palm.
One man delights if the volatile crowd
raise him up to triple honours; another rejoices
to store in his granary everything swept
from Libyan threshing floors.                                    10
Not even Attalian terms could ever seduce
to become a fear-fraught sailor,
to part Myrtoan sea with Cyprian keel,
the man who is glad to work with his hoe
his father's fields. The trader
fearing the south-west wind as it wrestles
th'Icarian swell, praises the calm of the wold
about his home town, yet soon will refurbish
his shattered bottoms, untaught to brook
privation. Others do not disdain cups                            20
of vintage Massic, nor to devote a substantial
part of the day to stretching their limbs
beneath the verdant arbutus or by
the quiet spring of some holy stream.
The camp, the sounding of trumpets mixed
with fifes, and the wars that mothers hate,
enthuse so many. The hunter stays out
under heaven's chill, forgetful of his wife,
whether faithful hounds have viewed a stag
or a Marsian boar may breach the fine-spun nets.                 30
But me the ivy guerdon on learnèd brows
ranks with the Gods above; me the cool copse

and grateful carols of Nymphs and Satyrs
dispart from the masses – provided Euterpe
does not withhold her flutes nor Polyhymnia
decline to tune the lyre of Lesbos:
and should you list me among the lyric bards
I shall nudge the stars with my lifted head.


## 2

### *Iam satis terris*

The Father has loosed upon earth sufficient
snow and hail, smitten with his livid
right hand the sacred heights and terrorized
    Rome our city,

terrorized all the peoples, lest Pyrrha's
burdensome age of prodigies come again,
when Proteus drove his seals to visit
    the high mountains,

and fishes lodged in the tops of elms
(till then well known as the haunt of doves),        10
and terrified does had to swim upon
    the whelming flood.

We saw the tawny Tiber (his waves
flung back with fury from the Tuscan shore)
advance to mine King Numa's palace
    and Vesta's shrine;

and boast he'd now avenge his Ilia (who protested
too much); and flow at large across
his own left bank (uxorious river)
    without Jove's consent.        20

Youth, made few by parents' vice, shall hear
of swords whetted for civil strife which better
had slain fell Parthians; shall hear
    of battles fought.

Which God shall the people call to affairs
of tottering empire? With what prayer shall
holy virgins beset pure Vesta not
    heeding their hymns?

To whom shall Jupiter assign the role
of atonement? Come at length, we pray,     30
prophetic Apollo, swathing in cloud
    your bright shoulder:

or you, smiling Venus, should it be your will,
around whom flutter both Joy and Desire:
or you if you care for neglected descendants,
    our sponsor Mars,

glutted on the long game, alas,
who delight in shouts and tossing helms
and fearsome Moorish infantry facing
    its bloody foes:     40

or you, winged Mercury, if changing
your shape you appear on earth as a youth
prepared to be named as avenger of
    Julius Caesar.

Then late return to the skies and long
be pleased to live among Romans: and though
our sins offend you, may no wind
    carry you away

betimes: here rather may you enjoy great
triumphs and the names of Father and Foremost     50
nor tolerate Parthian raids while you are
    our Leader, Caesar.

# 3

## *Sic te diva*

May the mighty Cyprian queen,
may Helen's brothers, shining stars,
    may the father of winds
(all bound bar Iapix) so helm you,

    ship, bearing in trust
our Virgil, that you render him unharmed,
    I pray, to Attic shores
and preserve the half of my soul.

    Oak and triple bronze
were about his breast who first committed       10
    his fragile boat
to the surly sea nor feared the headlong

    south-west wind fighting
it out with the north, nor moody Hyades,
    nor the south (the Adriatic's
chiefest judge) raising or laying the swell.

    What onset of death
did he fear who looked dry-eyed on floundering
    monsters, troubled seas
and the infamous skerry of Acroceraunia?      20

    The wise God sundered
the lands with estranging Ocean in vain
    since impious boats traverse
the sounds that ought to remain unstained.

    Boldly enduring all,
mankind rushes through sin and prohibition.
    Boldly Prometheus
by disobedient guile procured us fire:

and once that fire was brought
from its heaven-home, famine and a throng                    30
   of new fevers fell upon
earth; and death's necessity, hitherto slow

   and remote, now quickened
its pace. Daedalus tasted the empty air
   on wings not granted to men.
Hercules' efforts broke through Acheron.

   Nothing is too steep for man:
we foolishly seek for heaven itself, our sin
   will not let Jove
lay down his punitive thunderbolts.                    40

# 4

## *Solvitur acris hiems*

Sharp winter thaws for the spring and west wind,
   capstans haul down dry hulls,
flocks tire of the fold and the ploughman of the hearth,
   meadows no longer are blanched with frost.

Cytherea leads the dance by moonlight,
   the seemly Graces hand in hand
with Nymphs tread the rhythm while flamy Vulcan
   inspects the Cyclopes' gloomy works.

Now is the time to deck your glistening hair
   ¯with green myrtle or the flowers                    10
of the liberated Earth, to sacrifice to Faunus
   in the shady wood a lamb or a kid.

Pallid Death kicks impartially at the doors
   of hovels and mansions. O happy Sestius,
the brief sum of life invalidates long-term hopes.
   Soon night shall whelm you and fabled ghosts

and Pluto's mean home: once you are there the dice
    will deal you no mastery of wine or wonder
at tender Lycidas for whom all youths now burn
    and soon our virgins will kindle.                    20

# 5

## *Quis multa gracilis*

What slender boy besprinkled with fragrant oils
now crowds you, Pyrrha, amid the roses
in some convenient grotto?
For whom do you dress that yellow hair,

so simply neat? Alas, how often he will weep
at your and the Gods' vacillations –
oh he will be flabbergasted
by rough seas and black gales,

who now enjoys the illusion your worth is golden,
who supposes you will be always available, always        10
amiable, not knowing the breeze
deceives. I pity those

for whom you blandly glitter.
A votive plaque on the temple wall
shows damp clothes (mine) hung up
to the puissant God of the sea.

# 6

## *Scriberis Vario*

Varius the poet of Homeric flight
shall celebrate you as victorious, brave,
and the forces' exploits (marine or horse)
    under your command.

But I, too slight for grandeur, Agrippa
attempt nor that nor Peleus' son's high-stomached
no-surrender nor the voyaging about
    the seas of double-

dealing Ulysses nor Pelops' cruel house,
since Modesty and the pacific Muse                                10
forbid ineptitude lessen the praise of you and
    distinguished Caesar.

Who worthy to write of Mars his adamantine
coat, Meriones grimed with Trojan dust
or Tydides with Pallas' aid
    a match for the Gods?

Flippant as ever, whether afire
or fancy free, I sing of banquets and 'battles'
of eager girls with neatly trimmed nails
    against the young men.                                20

# 7

## *Laudabunt alii*

Let others praise bright Rhodes and Mytilene
    or Ephesus or the walls of twin-
bayed Corinth or Thebes renowned for Bacchus
    or Delphi for Apollo or Thessaly's Tempe.

There are whose one work is to celebrate in uncessant
    song the city of virgin Pallas and to wreathe
upon their brows olive sprigs gathered from far and wide.
    Many a one shall speak in Juno's honour

of Argos known for its steeds and of rich Mycenae.
    As for me, neither obdurate Sparta                    10
nor bounteous plain of Larisa has struck me so much
    as Albunea's booming cavern, and head-

long Anio, and Tibur's grove and orchards
    watered with frolicking streams.
As Notus often is bright and wipes the sky clean
    of shadowy clouds nor breeds perpetual

showers, so you, my Plancus, are wisely memorious
    to end life's dejection and burdens
with mellow wine, whether the camp refulgent with
    standards or your Tibur's dense shade                 20

now holds or shall hold you. Teucer fleeing from Salamis
    and his father, is said to have twined
around his wine-steeped head a poplar crown,
    addressing thus his grieving friends:

'Wheresoever Fortune (my father's better) shall bear us,
    there we shall go, my comrades and peers.
Under Teucer's fate and command, never abandon hope.
    Absolute Apollo has promised to Teucer

an unforeseeable Salamis in another country.
    O valiant men who with me have often                  30
suffered worse things, now drive out care with wine:
    tomorrow we take to the mighty sea.'

# 8

## *Lydia, dic, Per omnis*

Lydia, say, by all
the Gods I sue, why you make haste to kill
    Sybaris with love; why,
inured to dust and heat, he shirks the sun-baked plain;

    why rides no more
among his fellow cadets, nor curbs his Gallic mount
    with a tooth-edged bit.
Why does he funk the tawny Tiber? Why does he shun

    olive oil more
than vipers' blood, nor show his limbs livid     10
    from weapon practice,
who once hurled discus and javelin beyond the mark?

    Why does he hide
like sea-born Thetis' son before the grieving of Troy,
    lest masculine dress
should rush him to slaughter amid the Lycian squads?

# 9

## *Vides ut alta*

See how Soracte stands deep
in dazzling snow and the trees cannot bear
their loads and bitter frosts
have paralysed the streams.

Unfreeze, heap plentiful logs
on the hearth and produce
your four-year Sabine, Thaliarchus,
a fine and generous wine.

Commit all else to the Gods:
once they have quelled the mêlée                          10
of wind and churning water, cypress
and mountain ash will be still.

Avoid speculation
about the future; count as credit the days
chance deals; youth should not spurn
the dance or sweet desire;

this is your green time, not your white
and morose. In field or piazza,
now is the proper season for
trading soft whispers in the dark;                        20

the tell-tale complaisant laugh
of a girl in some secret nook;
the pledge removed from an arm
or a helpfully helpless finger.


# 10

## *Mercuri, facunde*

Atlas' trenchant grandson, Mercury,
whose wit first civilized new-made man
with the gift of speech and the cult of
        the wrestling-floor,

I sing of you, herald of Jove and all
the Gods, proponent of the curving lyre,
crafty to hide in klepto-jest whatever
        took your fancy.

Apollo threatened you as a child with his
frightening voice unless you gave back the cows    10
you'd magicked away, then laughed to find his
        quiver gone too.

Rich Priam leaving Ilium evaded
with your guidance the proud Atrides,
Thessalian watch-fires, the camp
    that menaced Troy.

And you bring in the dutiful souls
to the mansions of joy, direct the tenuous throng
with your golden wand, welcome alike to Gods
    above, below.                    20


# I I

## *Tu ne quaesieris*

Do not inquire, we may not know, what end
the Gods will give, Leuconoe, do not attempt
Babylonian calculations. The better course
is to bear whatever will be, whether Jove allot
more winters or this is the last which exhausts
the Tuscan sea with pumice rocks opposed.
Be wise, decant the wine, prune back
your long-term hopes. Life ebbs as I speak –
so seize each day, and grant the next no credit.


# I 2

## *Quem virum aut heroa*

What man or hero do you take up, Clio,
to proclaim on your lyre or incisive flute?
What God? What name will the teasing echo
    cause to resound

about Helicon's shady flanks
or upon cool Haemus' or Pindus' summit
(whence a forest mazèdly followed
        Orpheus singing,

who by his mother's art held back
the flowing of streams and rushing winds;                10
whose eloquent song and lyre drew away
        the spell-bound oaks)?

What should I speak before the accustomed praise
of the Father, who directs the affairs
of men and Gods, of sea and land
        and firmament,

who has created nothing greater than
himself, nor equal nor even proximate? Pallas,
brave in battle, has secured the esteem
        nearest to his,                                 20

however. And I will not omit to mention
you, Bacchus: nor the Virgin that's foe to wild
beasts: nor you, and fear of your flawless aim,
        archer Phoebus.

I shall speak of Alcides, and Leda's boys,
one famed as a horseman and one for
his boxing (as soon as their bright stars
        shine for sailors,

down from the reef pours the turbid sea,
the winds fade out, the clouds make off               30
and the menacing wave subsides because
        they will it so).

I am dubious whether to commemorate next
Romulus, Pompilius' peaceful reign, the arrogant
fasces of Tarquin or the celebrated
        death of Cato.

Regulus, the Scauri, and Paulus so prodigal
of his great spirit when Hannibal over-
came – these I rehearse in distinguished song.
   Fabricius too:       40

harsh poverty and patrimonial farms with
their homesteads raised apt for war
both him and longhaired Curius
   and Camillus.

The glory of Marcellus grows like a tree through
secluded generations. As the moon among lesser
lights, so the Julian constellation shines
   above others.

Father and guardian of the human race,
son of Saturn, to you the Fates have given  50
the care of mighty Caesar: you reign,
   and Caesar next.

After you he rules, with equity, Earth,
whether he leads in a just triumph
the Parthians tamed that threaten Rome
   or else, brought low,

the Indians and Seres of the Eastern borders:
yours with your heavy car to shake Olympus,
yours to launch down thunderbolts upon
   polluted groves.      60

# 13

## *Cum tu, Lydia*

 Lydia, when you praise
Telephus' rosy neck or Telephus'
 wax-white arms, alas,
my simmering liver swells with crotchety bile;

nor my mind nor complexion
are true to their nature, and stealthy tears
   on my cheeks are symptoms
of inward maceration above slow fires;

   and if some violent, drunken row
has marked your snowy shoulders or the ravening    10
   boy has stamped a memento
on your lips with his teeth, I am charred.

   You may not, let me tell you,
expect fidelity of the savage who injures
   that delicious mouth which Venus
has imbued with the essence of her nectar.

   Thrice happy the couple
who are not torn apart by quarrels
   but are held in a bond
of unbroken love which only death dissolves.    20


# 14

## *O navis, referent*

O ship, new waves will take you out to sea
once more. Then what to do? Valiantly
make for port. Do you not see that
your gunwales are stripped of oars,

and your splintered mast and yards
groan in the driving sou'wester, and without
any girding ropes your hull
can hardly survive the mightier

seas? You have no unsplit sails, nor Gods
to call upon when again beset by misfortune.    10
Though you're built of Pontic pine,
a daughter of a famous forest,

boastful of line and (ineffectual) name,
the fearful sailor has no faith in the icons
upon your stern. Beware lest you become
the laughing-stock of the winds.

Of late my acute disillusion but now
my concern and not inconsiderable love,
avoid the seas that rush betwixt
the glistening Cyclades.                              20

# 15

## *Pastor cum traheret*

When the faithless shepherd's Trojan ships
bore his hostess Helen over the sea,
Nereus blocked off the hastening winds
with an odious calm to prophesy

cruel fate: 'It is wrong to carry home one
whom many Greek warriors will strive to fetch back
and conspire to break your wedlock
and Priam's long-enduring realm.

Alas, what sweating of horses and men draws near!
How much bereavement you bring on the Trojan      10
people! Already Pallas prepares
her helmet, her shield, her chariot, her wrath.

In vain you shall comb your hair in Venus' tents
and sing to the cithara sweet divisions
to charm the female heart;
in vain you shall shun in your bedroom

the heavy spears, the arrows of Cretan cane,
the din of battle and Ajax hot
on your trail; you shall come (how late, alas)
to besmirch your adulterous locks in the dust.       20

Do you not heed Odysseus, the doom
of your line, nor Pylian Nestor?
Fearlessly Teucer of Salamis taxes
your strength; and Sthenelus skilled

in tactics and, if the need is to manage horses,
no sluggard charioteer. You shall know
Meriones too. And look, fell Tydides (his father's
better) rages to seek you out,

whom you, panting, head back, shall flee
as the deer forgetting its pasture flees                          30
the wolf espied across the glen –
whatever you promised your mistress.

The wrath of Achilles' Myrmidons may defer
the day of doom for Troy and the Trojan women,
but after th'appointed winters Achaean fires
shall raze the Asian homes.'


# 16

## *O matre pulchra*

O lovelier daughter of a lovely mother,
make what end you prefer
of my hurtful lines – on the fire,
in the sea, as you will.

Not Dindymene, nor the God in the Pythian
shrine when he shakes the priestess' mind,
nor Bacchus, nor the Corybantes
shrilling their cymbals,

are harsh as Anger, which neither Noric
swords deter nor the shipwrecking sea                             10
nor raging fire nor even Jove rushing
down in a fearful tempest.

It is said that Prometheus, obliged to add
to our primal substance particles drawn
from wherever, put in our stomachs
the urge of the ravening lion.

Anger laid Thyestes low in tragic
ruin and has always been the basic cause
why lofty cities have been razed
to the ground and conquering armies have          20

haughtily ploughed across their walls.
Govern your spirit: in sweet youth
heart's passion tried me too
and set me to raving

in rash lampoons. Now I would change
those acid lines for sweet, if only (since I take
back all my taunts) you'll be my friend
and give me back my heart.


# 17

## *Velox amoenum*

Swift Faunus often exchanges
Lycaeus for picturesque Lucretilis
to protect my flocks from the scorching
summer and rainy winds.

The rank billygoat's inconspicuous
wives in safety search the woods
for hidden arbutus and thyme,
nor do their kids fear virid snakes

nor the wolves of Mars whenever,
Tyndaris, Ustica's sloping valleys               10
and smooth-worn rocks have
resounded with that sweet piping.

The Gods are my guard, have at heart both
my worship and Muse. Here, lady,
shall a fruitful abundance of rustic glories
pour out for you from a lavish horn.

In this sequestered valley avoid
the Dog-Star's heat and sing to a Teian
lyre of Penelope and glass-green Circe
contending both for the one man;                    20

here in the shade receive innocuous
wine of Lesbos; Semele's Thyoneus shall not
engage in a fracas with Mars;
nor, watched over, need you fear

ineligible, insolent Cyrus
lest he lay on greedy hands,
lest he tear the garlands clinging
to your hair, or your inoffensive dress.


# 18

## *Nullam, Vare, sacra*

Varus, plant no tree before the sacred vine
about Catilus' walls and the fertile fields of Tibur:
the God proposes to the abstainer all things hard
and he alone dispels anxiety's stings.
Who after wine holds forth on poverty
and hard campaigns, rather than speaking
of father Bacchus and graceful Venus?
Lest anyone take too much of moderate Liber's gift,
be warned by the Centaurs' and Lapiths' brawl
that was fuelled and fought on unmixed wine;          10
be warned by Bacchus' disdain for the Thracians
when they distinguish right from wrong only
by their drunken passions' fine divide. Not I,
bright Fox's-Pelt, will wake you against your will

or expose to daylight your emblems dressed
in varied leaves. Restrain wild tambourines
and Berecyntian horns, which lead to blind 'love'
of self; to 'glory' lifting its empty head
unconsciously high; and to 'faith'
prodigal of secrets, transparent as glass.                    20


# 19

## *Mater saeva Cupidinum*

The Cupids' fierce mother
and Theban Semele's son with lickerish
    Licence command me
give heed once more to loves gone by.

Bright Glycera burns
gleaming more pure than Parian marble:
    her pretty frowardness
burns too dangerous to be beheld.

Venus entire rushing down
deserts her Cyprus, forbids me to sing                         10
    Scythians or Parthian cavalry
bold in flight or anything not to her point.

Here put living turf, here
foliage, slaves, and incense and a bowl
    of choicest two-year wine:
she'll come more kindly for sacrifice.

## 20

### *Vile potabis*

You'll drink a modest Sabine wine
from tankards – but I myself put it up
in Greek jars when in the Theatre
    the plaudits were yours,

sweet knight Maecenas, so that together
the banks of your native stream
and the joyous echo of Vatican Hill
    might return your praise.

You can imbibe Caecuban and wine
from Cales' press: but neither Falernian     10
vines nor Formian slopes shall
    replenish my cups.

## 21

### *Dianam tenerae*

You tender virgins, praise Diana;
you boys, praise longhaired
Apollo, and Latona entirely
loved by Jove in the highest.

Girls, praise her who delights in the streams
and the crests of the trees that stand out
on cool Algidus or in the dark woods
of Erymanthus and verdant Cragus.

Boys, give your praise to Tempe
and Apollo's birthplace Delos,     10
his shoulder marked out by his quiver
and the lyre contrived by his brother:

moved by your prayer, he shall drive
grievous war and pitiable famine and plague
off from our people and Caesar our prince
and on to the Parthians and Britons.

## 22

## *Integer vitae*

The man of upright life and free from sin
requires no Moorish spears nor bow
and quiver laden with poisoned
      arrows, Fuscus,

whether his route lies through
the sweltering Syrtes or inhospitable
Caucasus or regions the fabulous
      Hydaspes laps.

For as I wandered free from care
singing of Lalage in Sabine                                    10
woods, unarmed, beyond my bounds,
      there fled a wolf,

a monster such as warlike
Daunia does not rear in her widespread
groves of oak nor Juba's land, the barren
      nurse of lions.

Put me amid a limp plain where no
tree resurrects in the summer breeze,
a tract oppressed by Jupiter's haze
      and dingy sky;                                    20

put me in uninhabitable
regions beneath the Sun's close car –
and I'll love my Lalage's sweet talk
      and sweeter laugh.

# 23

## *Vitas inuleo*

You avoid me, Chloe, like a fawn
seeking his mother on the pathless
mountain and starting with groundless
fears at the woods and winds:

if the coming of spring shivers
the dancing leaves, or some green lizard
twitches a bramble,
his knees and heart quake.

Am I a tiger or fierce Gaetulian lion
to hunt you down and maul you?                    10
It is time to get loose from Mamma:
you are ripe for a man.

# 24

## *Quis desiderio*

What shame or limit to grief
for a life so dear? Teach sad laments
Melpomene to whom the Father
gave cithara and liquid voice.

And does sempiternal sleep oppress
Quintilius? When shall incorruptible Faith
(the sister of Justice) and Modesty
and naked Truth ever find his like?

Mourning for him aggrieves so many good men,
and none more mournful than you, my Virgil:    10
in vain, alas, you require of the Gods
Quintilius, whom loyal grief may not buy back.

What if you managed more sweetly
than Thracian Orpheus the lyre the trees heard?
Would blood then return to that vacant form
which with his harsh rod Mercury,

granting no prayer that fate be disclosed,
has herded into the darkling throng?
Severe: but patience may lighten
things we may not presume to change.                    20

# 25

## *Parcius iunctas*

The insistent blows of roistering youths
seldom rattle your shutters,
your sleep is unbroken, the door
    that moved its hinges

so smoothly once now clings to its
jamb. Now you hear less and less:
'Lydia, do you sleep while I expire for
    you the whole night long?'

A lonely crone in an alley, you in your turn
shall snivel for fornicators' disdain                    10
on moonless nights (the rising wind a
    bacchante from Thrace)

when the scorching love and lust
that more usually madden mares
shall rage about your liver.
    And you shall deplore

that pleasant young men take greater delight
in myrtle's pale- and ivy's dark-green
and consign dead leaves to Eurus,
    winter's companion.                    20

# 26

## *Musis amicus*

The Muses' friend, indifferent alike
to what king of the frozen Northern marches
is feared and to what now menaces
Tiridates, I shall consign

sadness and fear to unruly winds
to carry away across the Cretan sea.
Sweet Muse who delights in clear springs,
weave sunny flowers, oh weave a garland

for Lamia. For lacking you my tributes are
as nothing: fitting that you and your sisters　　　　　10
should celebrate him with new strings,
should sanctify him with Lesbos' plectra.

# 27

## *Natis in usum*

Throwing the cups about is behaviour
fit only for Thracians: abstain
from such barbarous habits, protect
seemly Bacchus from bloody brawls.

A Persian scimitar assorts
so grotesquely with wine and lamps – friends,
friends! – contain your blasphemous
clamour, lean back on your couches.

I too must drink up my ration of potent
Falernian? Then Megilla's brother shall tell us　　　　　10
with what wound he is beatified,
what arrow has made him droop.

You would rather not? I shall drink
on no other terms. Whichever Venus possess you,
she burns you with a fire which need
not make you blush and you sin

only with freeborn lovers. Come on, man –
whoever it is, you can trust our discretion.
Oh. Bad luck. In what a Charybdis
you flounder, you deserve a better flame.                    20

What witch or wizard with Thessalian drugs
can set you free – what God can, indeed?
Pegasus himself could hardly extricate you
from a tangle with the triple Chimaera.

# 28

## *Te maris et terrae*

A little mound of earth near the Matine shore
    contains you, Archytas, who measured
the sea, the land, the innumerable sands,
    and it avails you nothing

that you attempted the mansions of heaven and traversed
    with a mind born to die the polar rotund.
For Pelops' father died, though once a guest of the Gods;
    and Tithonus, translated to the winds;

and Minos, privy to the secrets of Jove; and Tartarus
    holds Euphorbus, consigned a second time           10
to Orcus, though by taking down the shield he witnessed
    to Trojan times and conceded to black

death nothing beyond his sinews and skin –
    in your opinion no mean critic
of nature and truth. But a common night awaits us,
    we all must walk death's path.

Some the Furies offer to bloody Mars as an
  entertainment; the hungry sea devours
sailors; obsequies for young and old contend for room;
  no head escapes cruel Proserpina.          20

The south wind, swift attendant of setting Orion, has over-
  whelmed me too in Illyrian waves.
Then sailor do not, from spite, begrudge the sifting sand:
  bestow a little upon my unburied bones

and skull. Then, whatever threats the east wind may vent
  against the Hesperian waves when Venusian forests
are beaten, may you be safe and a great reward, as it can,
  flow down to you from equitable

Jove and from Neptune the guardian of sacred Tarentum.
  Do you think it a small matter to do a wrong          30
that would harm your innocent children hereafter? Perhaps
  a right denied and outrageous misfortune are

lying in wait for *you*: my petition would not go unanswered,
  nor any amount of sacrifice redeem you.
I know you are impatient: the delay will not be long. Scatter
  three handfuls of earth and hurry away.


# 29

## *Icci, beatis*

Iccius, are you eyeing
Arabian treasures, preparing a dire foray
against Sabaean kings never before
conquered and forging fetters

for the gruesome Mede? What exotic
virgin, her fiancé killed, shall attend you?
What palace boy with unctuous curls,
taught to aim Eastern arrows

with his father's bow, shall be your
cupbearer? Who will deny that descending                    10
streams may well flow back to the heights
and Tiber reverse his course

when you, who promised so well, intend to swap
the illustrious books of Panaetius,
collected far and wide, plus
the Socratics, for a Spanish armour?


# 30

## *O Venus, regina*

O Venus, queen of Cnidos and Paphos, desert
the delights of Cyprus and come to the charming
shrine of Glycera who calls on you with
        so much incense.

Please hurry, and bring your hot-head son,
the Graces (their zones undone), and Nymphs,
and Youth (so ungracious when you're away),
        and Mercury.


# 31

## *Quid dedicatum*

What shall a poet ask of a consecrated
Apollo? What beg, as he pours young wine
from a dish? Not the rich cornfields
of fertile Sardinia,

nor the grateful herds of sultry
Calabria, nor India's ivory and gold,
nor land that the limpid waters of Liris
erode with silent flowing.

Let those appointed by Fortune prune the vines
with Calenian hooks that the wealthy merchant          10
may drink to the dregs from golden cups
the wine for which he trades Syrian goods:

he is dear to the Gods, for three or four times
each year he goes again upon the Atlantic
unscathed. My treat is olives,
endives and wholesome mallows.

Son of Latona, grant me I pray
to enjoy the things I have and my health
and to pass my old age with a sound
mind, with my cithara, and with style.                 20


# 32

## *Poscimur. Si quid*

A commission! If ever I have perpetrated
with you in the shade some trifle that lives
for this and future years, come sound a Latin
        poem, barbitos

first played by Lesbos' citizen who,
whether valiant between the weapons of war
or making fast his sea-flung boat
        on the streaming beach,

sang Bacchus, the Muses, and Venus
with her ever clinging boy,                             10
and personable Lycus's jetty
        eyes and jetty hair.

O badge of Phoebus, tortoise-shell lyre belov'd
at the banquets of Jove on high, o sweet and healing
surcease of distress, accept invocations
    conforming to lore.


# 33

## *Albi, ne doleas*

Tibullus, don't grieve overmuch to recall
inimical Glycera, don't keep on declaiming
lugubrious verses querying why, faith
broken, a younger man outshines you.

Love for Cyrus scorches Lycoris known
for her dainty forehead; Cyrus inclines
to waspish Pholoe; but sooner
shall she-goats go with Apulian wolves

than Pholoe err in shabby indiscretion.
This is Venus's way: her cruel humour         10
is pleased to subject to her yoke of bronze
incompatible bodies and minds.

Even I, when a better love sought me,
was detained in pleasant chains by Myrtale,
a one-time slave-girl more stormy than
Adriatic waves rolling round to Calabria.

# 34

## *Parcus deorum cultor*

A parsimonious and infrequent worshipper
of the Gods, adept of an ignorant
wisdom, I had gone astray, but now
have gone about, am forced to resume

the course I abandoned. Normally Jupiter
cleaves the clouds with his flashing fires,
but now he drove his thundering horses
and speeding chariot across a clear sky:

by which the dull earth, meandering streams,
and Styx, and hated Taenarus' waste home,                    10
and Atlas at the end of the world,
were shaken. The God has the power

to invert our zenith and nadir, raising obscurity,
lessening fame: rapacious Fortune
with shrill susurration removes his crown
from one, yet gladly grants it another.

# 35

## *O diva, gratum*

Goddess, Fortuna, ruler of pleasant Antium,
prompt to raise our mortal clay
from the lowest rank or transform
a pompous Triumph to a sad cortège,

you are entreated by the rustic
peasant's anxious prayer, as queen of the deep
by those who dare the Carpathian
sea in Bithynian ships,

by Dacian savages and Scythian refugees,
by cities and tribes and warlike Latium.                    10
The mothers of heathen kings,
and tyrants in purple fear

lest you unfairly kick down standing
pillars, and the thronging mob incite
('To arms!') the indecisive ('To arms!')
to challenge law and order.

Before you your servant Necessity stalks
with spikes and wedges in her brazen
hand, nor does she lack
the cruel hook or molten lead.                    20

Hope, and Loyalty swathed in white
attend you nor deny their allegiance
whenever you choose to desert
in mourning the homes of the great –

though the faithless rabble and perjured whore
turn away; and even friends, just
as fickle beneath the yoke of grief, disperse
when the jars are drained.

Preserve our Caesar, soon to go out
against ultimate Britain; preserve our young                    30
recruits, soon to plant fear in Eastern
realms and along the Arabian seaboard.

Alas, our scars and fratricides
shame us. What has this hard generation
balked at, what iniquity left
undone? From what have our youth

refrained through fear of the Gods?
What altars spared? Fortuna, reforge
against the Arabs and Massagetae
on new anvils our blunted swords.                    40

# 36

## *Et ture et fidibus*

With incense and lyres and
offerings of bullock's blood let us appease
  the Gods that guarded Numida
now safely returned from the furthest West,

  who distributes many kisses
among his peers, and on none more than on
  sweet Lamia, since he recalls
their boyhood under the selfsame tutor and

  manhood's toga assumed together.
So chalk it up against this blessèd day –                    10
  don't ration the wine-jugs,
don't rest your feet from the dance of Mars,

  and may our vinous Damalis not beat
Bassus at Thracian 'drinking-without-taking-breath',
  and let our feast lack neither
roses nor lingering parsley nor passing lilies.

  All shall cast their swooning
eyes on Damalis, but Damalis will not be torn
  from her love to whom
she clings more close than doting ivy.                        20

# 37

## *Nunc est bibendum*

Friends, now is the time to drink,
now tread the earth with our dancing,
now set Salian delicacies
before the Gods' couches.

Heretofore it had been a sin
to produce Caecuban from ancient racks,
while a crazy queen was plotting,
with her polluted train

of evil debauchees, to demolish
the Capitol and topple the Empire –                    10
a hopeful derangement drunk
with its luck. But the escape

from the flames of scarcely one ship
dampened her fury, and Caesar
dragged back to fearful reality
her mind swimming in Mareotic:

his galleys harried her fleeing from
Italy (just as the hawk the mild dove,
or the quick hunter the hare across
Thessaly's plains of snow), in order                    20

to put the curs'd monster in chains. Yet she,
seeking to die more nobly, showed
no womanish fear of the sword nor retired
with her fleet to uncharted shores.

Her face serene, she courageously viewed
her fallen palace. With fortitude
she handled fierce snakes, her corporeal
frame drank in their venom:

resolved for death, she was brave indeed.
She was no docile woman but truly scorned        30
to be taken away in her enemy's ships,
deposed, to an overweening Triumph.

# 38

## *Persicos odi*

I scorn these Persian preciosities, boy –
wreaths bound with linden bark, indeed,
and inquiries as to where the last rose
     is blowing.

It is misplaced zeal to elaborate
on simple myrtle. Here under trellised vines
myrtle is correct both for me drinking,
     you pouring.

# ODES

## BOOK II

# I

## *Motum ex Metello*

You treat of the civil troubles begun when Metellus
was consul, the causes of war, its blunders and phases,
the game of Fortune and the tragic amity
of great men and weapons smeared

with still unexpiated blood:
a task laden with perilous chances –
you proceed across fires
concealed beneath deceptive ashes.

May our theatres lack only briefly your Muse
of stern tragedy: soon, when you have chronicled          10
these affairs of state, take up once more
that lofty Athenian calling, Pollio,

celebrated shield of sad defendants,
pillar of the Senate's deliberations,
in whose Dalmatic Triumph
the laurel procured you eternal fame.

Meanwhile you draw our ears
with the menacing blare of horns; tuckets resound;
the flashing of weapons strikes alarm
into nervous horses and the horsemen's faces.          20

Even now I seem to hear mighty captains
(grimed with not inglorious dust)
and all the world subdued
except the fierce heart of Cato.

Now Juno and the Gods who inclined to Numidia
but were forced to desert her take their revenge
by offering on Jugurtha's grave
his conquerors' grandsons.

What plain is not enriched with Latin blood
to witness with its graves to our unholy                    30
wars, the resounding fall of the West
audible even to Parthian ears?

What eddy or stream untainted
by the shameful war? What sea
is not incarnadined with Apulian blood?
What shore has no news of our slaughters?

—But lest you leave your pleasantries,
insouciant Muse, to attempt again a Cean dirge,
come seek with me in some Dionean ravine
music in a more cheerful mode.                    40


## 2

# *Nullus argento*

There is no lustre to silver concealed
in the greedy ground, Sallustius Crispus,
you foe to metal unless it shine
           from rational use.

Proculeius shall survive long ages, known
as a father towards his brothers;
lasting Fame shall bear him up on wings
           that refuse to droop.

You shall rule a larger realm by subduing
your own acquisitive heart than by joining Libya                    10
to distant Gades, the Punic both sides
           to serve only you.

Dire dropsy swells by feeding, and thirst
is not quenched until the disease's cause
has fled from the veins and watery dullness
           from the pallid flesh.

Virtue, dissenting from the mob, declines to
number Phraates among the bless'd, though restored
to Cyrus's throne, and teaches the people
      to call things by their                               20

right names, granting power, a secure crown
and especial laurels only to the man who can gaze
on mountains of treasure without glancing.
      over his shoulder.


# 3

## *Aequam memento*

Dellius, all must die: be sure to retain
an equable mind in vexation
avoiding also intemperate joy
at advantages gained,

whether you lead a life of gloom
or relax stretched out on some sequestered
lawn throughout the holy days
and rejoice in classic Falernian wine.

Why do the pines and silvery poplars
share their hospitable shade?                                10
Why does runaway water
tremble in winding streams?

With us, for us. Command all perfumes, wines
and the too brief spell of the rose
while affairs and times
and the Fates' black thread allow:

then goodbye freehold woodlands, home
and the manor the yellow Tiber washed
and the spoils piled up to the heights,
which your heir shall get.                                   20

Rich man born from ancient Inachus
or poor man, it makes no odds, from the lowest
race under sky you shall fall
Orcus's victim, who pities none.

All are thus compelled;
early or late the urn is shaken;
fate will out; a little boat
shall take us to eternal exile.

# 4

## *Ne sit ancillae*

No need to blush because you love
a slave-girl, Xanthias. By way of precedent,
the snowy skin of Briseis
    moved Achilles;

the beauty of Tecmessa moved her
master Ajax; Agamemnon himself
in the midst of triumph burned for
    a captive girl

when barbarian hosts went down
before Thessaly's victor and Hector's fall          10
brought forward for the weary Greeks
    the sack of Troy.

For all you know your blonde Phyllis's parents
would lend their son-in-law lustre – surely
a line of kings, and she grieves at her
    Gods' unfairness.

Believe me, she is no wretched pleb
and a girl so loyal and averse to profit
was not born of a mother you would
    not want to know.          20

(I praise her arms, her face and her
full calves chastely: avoid
suspicion of one who is already
    forty years old.)


# 5

## *Nondum subacta*

She has not yet the strength to submit
to the double yoke and manage her part
or bear the weight of a bull
    plunging in venery.

The mind of your heifer is given
to green fields, now easing her stifling
warmth in the brook, now longing
    to play with the calves in marshy

willow-groves. Forswear desire
for unripe grapes: soon varicoloured       10
Autumn will paint your
    darkening clusters purple.

Soon she will woo: injurious time
makes haste and adds to her those years
it takes from you. Soon froward
    Lalage will seek a husband

delectably – more so than fugitive
Pholoe; than Chloris, whose snowy
shoulder gleams like the purest moon
    on the sea by night;            20

than Cnidian Gyges, who if placed
in a group of girls would deceive
a shrewd stranger by his flowing
    hair and ambiguous face.

# 6

## *Septimi, Gades aditure*

Septimius, ready to go with me to Gades;
to Cantabria, untaught to bear our yoke;
to the barbarous Syrtes where Moorish
        waves forever seethe:

if only Tibur founded by Argive settlers
might be the haven of my old age,
my goal when fatigued at last with seas,
        with roads, with campaigns!

And if the Parcae ban me there, I shall make
for Galaesus' river that's dear to skin-                    10
clad sheep, and the countryside ruled by
        Spartan Phalanthus.

That parcel of land smiles for me
above all others, where the honeys will not cede
to Hymettus and the olives still vie
        with green Venafrum;

where Jupiter proffers early springs
and mild winters, and Aulon the friend
of fruitful Bacchus hardly envies
        Falernian grapes.                                   20

That place with its blessèd heights
summons both you and me, and there shall you
asperge with tears the still warm ashes of
        your friend the poet.

# 7

## *O saepe mecum*

O my friend and oldest comrade,
with whom I have often seen out
the vinous, lagging day,
with Syrian myrrh in my hair;

Pompeius, so often led with me
into extremity by our general
Brutus; who has restored you
to citizenship, your native

Gods and Italian skies? With you I knew
the rout at Philippi and my shield,                          10
to my shame, left behind
where manhood failed and words

were eaten. Luckily Mercury
bore me away, in my fright, in a cloud:
but the undertow sucked you back
to the weltering straits of war.

Now render to Jove the banquet pledged:
lay your frame, fatigued with long
campaigns, beneath my laurel nor spare
the jars set aside for this day.                             20

Fill the bright cups with Massic
oblivion, pour scent from capacious
shells. Who will contrive our
crowns of myrtle and moist

parsley? Whom will the dice make master
of wine? I shall drink deep
as Edonians do: it is sweet
to rave for a friend restored.

# 8

## *Ulla si iuris*

Had your perjuries ever been
punished, Barine; had a tooth
turned black, perhaps; had you even
    broken a nail;

I could trust you now. But you give
your (fallacious) word, and your beauty
shines yet brighter, the cynosure
    of Roman youth.

You find that it pays to swear
'By my mother's ashes!' – 'By the silent        10
stars in the sky!' – 'Witness the Gods,
    whom no death chills!'

And Venus herself, and cruel Cupid
sharpening his poisoned darts on a bloody
stone, and even the simple Nymphs, are
    obliged to smile.

Added to which our freeborn boys
are growing up in effect your slaves;
nor can your older fans bear to jilt
    their lying love.                20

Mothers and thrifty elders fear
for their sons on account of your name,
and newlywed brides suspect their
    husbands detained.

# 9

## *Non semper imbres*

The clouds don't always pour down showers
on the sodden farmland nor choppy squalls forever
perturb the Caspian sea, friend Valgius;
the numbing ice of Armenian marches

does not obdure the whole year through;
Garganus' oak-groves do not strive
against the north wind and ash-trees
are not stripped of foliage permanently.

Yet you incessantly rehearse in dying falls
the loss of Mystes: your love-laments      10
do not desist when Vesper rises,
or fades before the rushing sun.

He who survived three generations
did not mourn through all his life his belov'd
Antilochus; nor did his Phrygian parents
and sisters weep without term for their boy

Troilus. Then cease at last
your tender complaining –
let us rather sing of Augustus Caesar's
new trophies; the ice-bound Niphates;      20

the Parthian river swirling in lesser eddies
now it is added to the conquered realms;
the Geloni riding within prescribed
limits across their narrowed plains.

## 10

## *Rectius vives*

The proper course in life, Licinius,
is neither always to dare the deep, nor,
timidly chary of storms, to hug
    the dangerous shore.

Who values most the middle way
avoids discreetly both the squalor
of the slum and a palace liable
    to excite envy.

The gale shakes most the lofty pine,
tall towers fall with the louder           10
crash and the highest peaks most often
    are struck by lightning.

Hopeful in evil times and cautious
in good, ready for weal or woe,
be prepared. Jupiter imposes
    the ugly winter,

but then withdraws it. Bad luck
is not for ever: Apollo varies
his archery sometimes by harping
    to waken the Muse.           20

In difficult straits show spirit
and fortitude, but on the other hand
always shorten sail when you
    run before the wind.

## I I

## *Quid bellicosus*

Forbear to inquire, Quinctius Hirpinus,
what bellicose Cantabrians, and Scythians
removed from us by the Adriatic interposed,
are plotting. Do not excruciate about

the modest needs of life: fresh youth
and beauty recede behind us; drouth
and wrinkles ban amorous longing
and the knack of easily falling asleep.

The glory of vernal flowers is not
for ever, nor does the bright moon shine                10
with one sole face. Why tire your mortal mind
with counsels of eternity?

Better to drink while we may,
reclining insouciant beneath some
lofty plane or pine, greybeards wreathed
in fragrant roses, anointed

with Syrian nard. Bacchus dissipates
nagging cares. Which slave shall quickly
temper at the passing brook
the bowls of hot-blooded Falernian?                     20

Who shall lure from her home the shy drab
Lyde? Go tell her to hurry, and come
with her hair neatly knotted Laconian-
style, and bring her ivory lyre.

## 12

### *Nolis longa ferae*

You'd not wish fierce Numantia's tedious wars
or doughty Hannibal or the Sicilian sea scarlet
with Carthaginian blood to be adapted to
the cithara's gentle measures,

nor Hylaeus and the Lapiths fighting drunk,
nor the sons of the Earth subdued by
Hercules' hand, whence peril
made tremble the shining house

of ancient Saturn: you would tell better
in narrative prose, Maecenas,                                    10
of Caesar's campaigns and hostile kings
led haltered through the streets.

The Muse has commanded me to speak
of your lady Licymnia's mellifluous
singing, her softly flashing eyes,
her heart so faithful in mutual love.

Joining in with the choral dancers
or bandying jokes or going arm in arm
in the press of bright virgins on Diana's
holy day, her grace was not diminished.                          20

Would you trade a lock of Licymnia's hair
for all that rich Achaemenes owned,
the Mygdonian wealth of fertile Phrygia,
or the chock-full homes of Arabia,

when she bends her neck to your glowing
kisses, or (gently stubborn) denies you, since
(more than you wooing) she likes to have them
stolen, and sometimes she steals first?

# 13

## *Ille et nefasto*

It was a black day when whoever it was
first planted you, tree, and raised you
sacrilegiously to posterity's
mishap and shame of the parish.

I could well believe that he strangled
his father and spattered the hearth
at night with the blood of
a guest. The man who set you up

had dabbled in Colchic poisons
and all sins everywhere ever invented,                    10
you wretched stump who fell on the head
of your unoffending master.

Man never studies enough, from hour
to hour, of what he should be ware:
the Punic sailor abhors the Bosph'rus, but no
unforeseeable fate elsewhere;

the soldier the arrows of Parthians
swiftly retreating; the Parthians Roman chains
and dungeons; yet the violent deaths are unforeseen
that sweep and will sweep away the peoples.              20

How near I came to seeing the realms
of shadowy Proserpina, Aeacus giving judgement,
the allotted mansions of the righteous,
and Sappho with her Aeolian lyre

complaining of the girls of her country,
and you, Alcaeus, more forcefully
musicking hardship at sea,
hardship in exile, the hardship of war –

the shades must wonder at both pronouncing
things worthy of reverent silence, but the dense          30
mob shoulder to shoulder drinks in more
of battles and tyrants put out.

No wonder, when mesmerized by such songs,
that the hundred-headed beast lays back
his ears, and the snakes that writhe
in the Furies' hair fall still in rest.

The soothing sounds bring even Prometheus
and Tantalus delusive respite from torment,
and Orion feels no urge
to harry the lions or nervous lynxes.                      40


# 14

## *Eheu fugaces*

Postumus, Postumus, fleeting years
glide swiftly by, virtue can give no pause
to wrinkles or imminent age
or invincible death –

no, not if you seek to placate
with three hundred bulls each day
Pluto who relentlessly jails
Tityos and threefold Geryon

within that grimly circling river
all must traverse who thrive                               10
by the spilth of earth, be we kings
or substanceless peasants.

In vain we keep away from bloody Mars
and griding Adriatic breakers,
in vain avoid the autumnal south wind
that is foe to flesh and blood:

we needs must look on winding black
Cocytus' sluggish stream, Danaus' infamous
brood and Sisyphus son of Aeolus,
condemned to long labour.                               20

Earth, home and kindly wife
must be left, nor will any of the trees
you foster, except the unloved cypress,
follow their brief master.

A worthier heir shall consume your Caecuban
preserved with a hundred keys and drench
the pavement with a fine wine
too good for priestly banquets.


# 15

## *Iam pauca aratro*

Now regal villas will leave few acres
for ploughing; on all sides ornamental ponds
will appear as extensive
as Lake Lucrinus; bachelor plane-trees

usurp the elm; beds of violets
and myrtles and all olfactory crops
scatter their scents in olive-groves
which previous owners farmed;

dense laurels exclude the burning strokes
of the sun. This is not the norm                        10
our ancestors divined, that Romulus
and rough-bearded Cato prescribed.

For them private wealth was small,
the commonweal great: no private
north-facing shady porches
were then laid out with ten-foot rules:

the law forbade abuse of the common turf
and enjoined the adornment at public expense
of the towns and temples
with fresh-hewn marble.                                    20


# 16

## *Otium divos*

Peace, Grosphus, is what the man on the open
Aegean requires of the Gods when black cloud
obscures the moon and no fixed star can
        flash for the sailors.

Peace for the Thracians enraged with war,
peace for the Medes with their stylish quivers,
is not to be bought with gems or gold
        or gleaming fabrics.

Neither Persian treasure nor the consul's
lictor can disperse the wretched mob                       10
of the mind or the cares that flit about
        your coffered ceilings.

He lives well on a little whose family
salt-cellar shines amid a modest
table, whose gentle sleep is not dispelled
        by fear or base greed.

Why do we aim so high, so bravely,
so briefly? Why hanker for countries scorched
by an alien sun? What exile from home
        can avoid himself?                                 20

Care clambers aboard the armoured ships,
keeps pace with the cavalry squadrons, comes
swift as east-wind-driven rain, comes
        swift as any stag.

The soul content with the present
is not concerned with the future and tempers
dismay with an easy laugh. No
    blessing is unmixed.

An early death snatched bright Achilles;
long senility reduced Tithonus:                    30
this hour will offer to me, maybe, the good
    it denies to you.

For you a hundred herds of Sicilian
cattle moo; for you are bred
neighing mares apt for the chariot;
    you dress in twice-dyed

Tyrian purple wool: to me honest Fate
has given a little farm, the delicate breath
of the Grecian Muse, and disdain
    for the jealous mob.                    40


# 17

## *Cur me querelis*

Why do you stifle me so with complaining?
It is neither my will nor that of the Gods
that I should die before you, Maecenas,
you glory and mighty prop of my affairs.

If some untimely blow should take you,
the half of my heart, ah, why should I linger,
neither loved as before nor surviving
whole? The selfsame day shall bring

us both our doom. I have taken
no false oath: we shall go, we shall go,                    10
whenever you lead the way, comrades prepared
to take the last journey together.

No fiery breath of Chimaera, nor hundred-
handed Gyas, should he rise in our way,
shall ever tear me from you; this is the will
of the Fates and of mighty Justice.

Whether formidable Scorpio, or Libra,
or Capricorn (lord of the Western sea)
oversaw with more powerful
influence my nativity,                                        20

your stars and mine accord in the most
incredible manner. The protection of Jove,
outshining baleful Saturn,
rescued you and hindered the wings

of impatient Fate when the thronging public
in the Theatre broke three times into glad applause:
a tree-trunk falling on my head
would have made away with me had not Faunus,

the guard of Mercurial men, warded off the blow
with his hand. Remember to offer                             30
a votive shrine with victims:
and I will sacrifice a humble lamb.


# 18

## *Non ebur neque aureum*


No ivory or gilded
panels gleam in my house; no
   beams from Hymettus
press on columns quarried in Africa's

   heartland; I have not
unexpectedly inherited a palace from Attalus;
   I have no retinue
of ladies trailing Laconian purple

robes. I am loyal, however,
and of a kindly humour: though poor,                          10
   am courted by the rich. Content
with my Sabine farm, I make no more suits

   to my powerful friend,
seek nothing further from the Gods above.
   Each day drives out the day
before, new moons make haste to wane:

   yet you, on the brink of the grave,
contract for the cutting of marble slabs;
   forgetful of death you fret
to build your mansion out from the coast            20

   in the roaring sea at Baiae –
the mainland shore will not suffice.
   What do you hope to achieve
by tearing down fences and avidly

   jumping your tenants'
boundaries? Men and women are evicted,
   clutching to their breasts
both household Gods and ragged children.

   And yet no hall more certainly
awaits the rich grandee than does rapacious          30
   Orcus' predestined
bourne. What more can you need? Earth

   opens impartially for paupers
and the sons of kings, and Charon could not
   be bribed to ferry back
even resourceful Prometheus. He holds

   Tantalus and Tantalus'
progeny, and whether or not invoked
   is alert to disburden
the serf when his labour is done.                         40

# 19

## *Bacchum in remotis*

I have seen Bacchus amid far rocks
(believe me, posterity)
teaching paeans to attentive Nymphs
and goat-foot Satyrs with pointed ears.

Evoe! My heart is thrilled with awe still new
and wildly rejoices, my breast is so full
of Bacchus. Evoe! Spare me, spare me,
Liber, so feared for your rigorous rod.

My holy task is to sing of the unremitting
Bacchantes, rehearse the spring of wine,          10
the brooks of rich milk and the honey
dropping from hollow trees;

my holy task your deified queen's reward
among the stars, the palace of Pentheus
overturned in grievous ruins, eradication
of Thracian Lycurgus.

You control rivers, you the savage sea;
on the distant ridges, euphoric,
you bind the hair of Bistonian
women with harmless vipers;          20

you, when the mutinous company of Giants
would climb steep-up to the realms of the Father,
put on the terrible lion's claws
and fangs and hurled back Rhoetus.

Though held to be more fit for dancing,
jokes and games, not competent
for battle, yet you have been
in the thick of war as well as at peace.

Cerberus saw you comely with your golden horn
and did not harm you, but mildly                              30
wagged his tail, and as you passed he lightly
touched your feet with his triple tongue.


# 20

# *Non usitata*

A bard, I shall travel two-formed
in the clear aether upon no common
or feeble wings, nor linger
on earth, nor (bigger than envy)

desert the City. I, whose blood is
of indigent stock, I, whom you invite,
belovèd Maecenas, shall never perish
nor be confined by the waves of Styx.

Already dry skin becomes the norm
on my shins, on top I transmogrify                           10
to a white swan, soft down begins
to appear on my fingers and shoulders.

Soon, a melodious bird, more known
than Icarus son of Daedalus, I shall view
the Hyperborean prairies, the Syrtes,
the Bosphorus' sighing seashore.

Colchians, Dacians (dissimulating fear
of our Marsian cohorts) and remote Geloni
shall come to study me, by glossing me
Spaniards and drinkers of Rhône grow wise.                   20

Omit from my delusive funeral rites
the dirge and ugly grief and lamentations:
restrain all outcry, forgo
the bootless tribute of a tomb.

# ODES

## BOOK III

# I

## *Odi profanum vulgus*

I shun and keep removed the uninitiate crowd.
I require silence: I am the Muses' priest
and sing for virgins and boys
songs never heard before.

Dread kings rule over their own,
but over those kings is the rule of Jove,
famed for the Giants' defeat,
governing all by the lift of his eyebrow.

It is true that one man plants vineyards larger
than his neighbour's; that in the Campus                    10
one candidate for office is of nobler blood;
another of greater reputation

and worth; another has a bigger crowd
of retainers: but with impartial justice
Necessity chooses from high and low,
the capacious urn shuffles every name.

Sicilian feasts will distil
no sweet savour, nor will the music
of birds and citharas restore
his sleep above whose neck                                  20

the drawn sword hangs: soft sleep
does not disdain the cottages
of rustics nor the shady bank
nor Tempe fanned by Zephyrs.

Tumultuous seas and the furious onset
of setting Arcturus or rising Haedus
do not deter the man
who desires no more than his needs –

not by lashing his vines with hail,
nor by fickle farmland, the trees                    30
now blaming the floods, now stars
that parch the field, now hostile winter.

Fishes perceive the sea diminished
by foundations laid in the deep: here
the contractor and thronging slaves
and the master disdaining the land

lower stones. But Fear and Threats arise
to the selfsame mark as the owner, nor does
black Care quit the bronze-beaked trireme
and even mounts behind the horseman.                 40

If neither Phrygian marbles nor purples
more lustrous than starlight
nor Falernian vines nor Persian nards
can comfort one grieving,

why should I construct a lofty hall
in the latest style with enviable pillars;
why would I change my Sabine dale
for burdensome wealth?


# 2

## *Angustam amice*

Let the healthy boy learn to suffer
strait poverty gladly in hard campaigns;
as lancer molest with his point
the barbarous Parthian natives

and lead a fresh air life amid perilous
undertakings. From enemy ramparts
a queen and her daughter shall groan
for some struggling tyrant:

'Dear husband and father, alas,
unseasoned in warfare, do not provoke                    10
with a touch that bloody lion
berserk amid the slaughter!'

It is sweet and proper to die for one's country
and death harries even the man who flees
nor spares the hamstrings or cowardly
backs of battle-shy youths.

Manhood ignores the smear of outvoting
and shines with unalloyed esteem,
nor assumes nor resigns the fasces
at the waftings of public opinion.                    20

Manhood reveals their heaven to those
who deserve not to die, attempts the narrow pass,
and spurns with its soaring wings
the common crowd, the muddy ground.

Safe the recompense likewise of loyal
tact: who broadcasts the mysteries of Ceres
shall be forbidden to lie beneath
the same timbers or sail the same dinghy

as me – slighted, the Ancient of Days is apt
to confuse the innocent with the guilty:                    30
though lame in one foot, Retribution
rarely abandons the Sinner's trail.


# 3

## *Iustum et tenacem*

The just man tenacious of his purpose
will not be shaken from his set resolve
by the inflamed citizenry demanding wrong,
nor by the impending face of a tyrant, nor Auster

the troubled master of the restless Adriatic,
nor the mighty hand of thundering Jove:
were the sky itself to fracture and collapse,
the wreckage would immolate him unafraid.

By such address both Pollux and roving Hercules
aspired to and reached the starry citadels,                    10
reclining with whom Augustus shall
sip nectar with empurpled lips.

On account of such merit, father Bacchus,
you were conveyed by tigers bearing yokes
on untamed necks; and you, Quirinus,
with Mars's steeds escaped from Acheron

as Juno in the Gods' council
enounced the welcome speech: 'Ilium, Ilium
has been reduced to dust
by a fated, partial judge                                      20

and a foreign woman: for since Laomedon
cheated the Gods of their contracted pay
the city with its people and treacherous king
has been forfeit to me and to chaste Minerva.

The egregious guest no longer dazzles
his Spartan adulteress, nor can the perjured house
of Priam with Hector adjuvant
throw back the besieging Greeks:

the war that our vendettas prolonged
is now resolved. Henceforth my great wrath                     30
is at an end. I shall restore to Mars
my hateful grandson the Trojan

priestess bore: I shall suffer him
to enter the abodes of light,
to imbibe the quickening nectar,
to be enrolled in the Gods' calm ranks.

As long as broad ocean seethes between
Troy and Rome, let the bless'd exiles rule
wherever they will; as long as cattle trample
the memorials of Paris and Priam                    40

where beasts with impunity hide
their cubs, so long may the gleaming Capitol
stand and brave Rome dictate terms
to the Medes and subject them to Triumphs:

feared far and wide, let her name extend
to ultimate borders where intervening waters
part Europe from the Moors; where Nile
by flooding irrigates the fields.

Let her be stronger by spurning at unprospected gold
(and better so located, concealed in earth)           50
than by mining it out for human use
with hands that plunder all things sacred.

Whatever limit bounds the world
may her forces reach it, eager to view
both the frenzied dancing of heat
and mists and veils of rain.

But the fate of the warlike Romans is subject
to one condition: let them not,
too loyal, and confident of gain,
wish to restore the roofs of ancestral Troy.           60

Should the fortunes of Ilium be reborn,
evil omens and woeful slaughter
shall come again and I, Jove's queen
and sister, shall lead the invading hosts.

Should walls of bronze arise three times
by Phoebus' power, thrice shall my Argives
lay them low and destroy them, thrice shall
the captive wife weep for her husband and sons.'

– But these things do not suit my cheerful lyre:
Muse, where are you bound? Cease doggedly          70
to report the debates of the Gods,
to trivialize great themes with little metres.


# 4

## *Descende caelo*

Come down from heaven, Calliope, articulate
on the flute a melody long drawn out,
or with your incisive voice, if you prefer,
or upon the strings of Phoebus' cithara.

– Do you hear her, or does an amiable
delusion mock me? I seem to hear,
and to wander through sacred groves
where soothing waters and breezes rise.

On pathless Vultur, beyond the threshold
of my nurse Apulia, when I was exhausted          10
with play and oppressed with sleep,
legendary wood-doves once wove for me

new-fallen leaves, to be
a marvel to all who lodge in lofty
Acherontia's eyrie and Bantia's woodlands
and the rich valley farms of Forentum,

as I slept with my flesh secure
from bears and black snakes, covered
with holy laurel and gathered myrtle,
a brave child by the Gods' assent.          20

Yours, my Muses, yours, I climb
to the Sabine heights, or visit cool
Praeneste or hillside Tibur
or lucent Baiae, just as I feel inclined:

neither the broken line at Philippi,
nor that cursèd tree, nor Sicilian seas
off Palinurus' cape, have quite destroyed me,
a friend to your springs and choirs.

Whenever you go with me,
I shall gladly attempt as sailor                                    30
the raving Bosphorus, as voyager
the scorching sands of Syrian shores;

shall visit the Britons savage to guests,
the Concanian merry on horses' blood,
shall visit unscathed the quiver-
bearing Geloni, the Scythian stream.

It is you who refresh high Caesar
in some Pierian grotto when he seeks
to rest from his labours, and has billeted
in the towns his campaign-weary legions.                          40

You give calm wisdom, kindly ones,
and having given, rejoice. We know
how the mutinous Titans and their foul
horde suffered the falling thunderbolt

of him who controls still earth, the wind-
swept sea, the cities, the realms of the dead,
who rules alone with equitable power
both the Gods and the throngs of mortals.

That arrogant progeny bristling with hands
and the brothers striving to heap                                  50
Pelion on shadowy Olympus
inflicted great fear on Jove.

But what could Typhoeus do, or powerful Mimas,
what Porphyrion, for all his menacing posture,
what Rhoetus, or Enceladus,
brave hurler of tree-trunks uprooted,

by charging against the resounding shield
of Minerva? Here stood avid
Vulcan, here matronly Juno and he
who shall never leave bow from shoulder                    60

and washes his waving hair in pure
Castalian dew, who keeps his native woods
and the Lycian thickets,
Patara's and Delos' Apollo.

Force without polity falls by its weight:
force directed the Gods themselves
make greater – but force that cogitates
in its heart fell sin, they loathe.

(Hundred-handed Gyas be witness
to my maxims, and Orion the known                    70
assailant of chaste Diana,
but tamed by the virgin's arrows.)

Heaped on her monsters, Earth mourns
and laments the offspring the thunderbolt sent
to ashen Orcus; nor has the quick
fire eaten through Aetna superimposed;

nor does the vulture (set to guard
his iniquity) relinquish the liver
of immoderate Tityos; and three hundred chains
hold fast the amorous Pirithous.                    80


# 5

## *Caelo tonantem*

His thunder confirms our belief that Jove
is lord of heaven; Augustus shall be held
an earthly God for adding to the Empire
the Britons and redoubtable Parthians.

Did Crassus' troops live in scandalous
marriage to barbarians (o Senate,
and custom perverted), grow old
bearing arms for alien fathers-in-law;

did Marsians, Apulians, under a Parthian
king, forget the sacred shields,                                    10
the name, the toga, and immortal Vesta;
while Jove and his city Rome were unharmed?

The provident mind of Regulus was ware
of this when he rejected shameful terms,
extrapolating catastrophe in time
to come from such a precedent

unless the captured youths should
perish unpitied. 'I myself have seen
our standards affixed to Punic shrines,'
he said, 'with the weapons wrested                                    20

from our soldiers and no blood spilt; I myself
have seen the arms of free men, citizens,
twisted back, the gates of Carthage open,
the fields we ravaged worked again.

Ransomed with gold our cohorts will, of course,
re-form with heightened morale . . . To shame
you add expense. The wool that's treated with dye
will never resume the colours it lost;

nor does manhood, once it has lapsed,
consent to lodge in less than men.                                    30
When the doe disentangled from close-
meshed nets puts up a fight, then will he

be brave who entrusted himself to treacherous foes;
and he will trample Carthage in another war
who has tamely felt the thongs
on his pinioned arms, and dreaded death.

Not knowing whence he draws his life, he
has confounded peace and war. Obscene!
O mighty Carthage, more sublime
by Rome's opprobrious downfall!'                    40

They say that like an outlaw
he put aside his chaste wife's kiss
and little children and sternly lowered
his manly gaze to the ground,

hoping to steady the vacillating Senate
by counsel never given before,
and hurried out among his grieving
friends an unexampled exile.

He knew very well what the alien
torturers proposed. Nevertheless,               50
he parted the kinsmen blocking his path
and the crowd delaying his going,

as though, some tedious law-suit settled,
he were leaving his clients' affairs
in order to travel amid Venafran fields
or perhaps to Spartan Tarentum.

# 6

## *Delicta maiorum*

Though innocent you shall atone for the crimes
of your fathers, Roman, until you have restored
the temples and crumbling shrines of the Gods
and their statues grimy with smoke.

Acknowledge the rule of the Gods – and rule:
hence all things begin, to this ascribe the outcome.
Contemned, the Gods have visited many
evils on grieving Hesperia.

Already twice Monaeses and Pacorus' band
have crushed our ill-starred offensive                    10
and preen themselves on having added
Roman spoils to their paltry gauds.

Our city busied with sedition has almost
suffered destruction by Egypt allied to Dacia,
the former renowned for her fleet, the latter
rather for hurtling arrows.

Teeming with sin, the times have sullied
first marriage, our children, our homes:
sprung from that source disaster has whelmed
our fatherland and our people.                    20

The grown girl loves to be taught to be
artful and dance oriental dances,
obsessed to her dainty fingernails
with illicit amours.

She sniffs out young philand'rers at her
husband's feast, nor is she nice to choose
to whom she (hurriedly) grants her favours
when the lamps are removed,

but brazenly stands when called – with her
husband's assent – though some travelling                    30
salesman or Spanish ship's captain
may be the agent of Shame.

The generation that dyed the Punic
sea with blood and laid low Pyrrhus,
Antiochus and Hannibal was not born
of parents such as these,

but of manly comrades, yeoman soldiers
taught to turn the soil with Sabine hoes
and carry cut firewood at a strict
mother's bidding when the Sun                    40

advanced the shadows of the hills
and lifted the yokes from weary steers,
his departing chariot leading in
the hours of comfort.

What does corrupting time not diminish?
Our grandparents brought forth feebler heirs;
we are further degenerate; and soon will beget
progeny yet more wicked.

# 7

## *Quid fles, Asterie*

Asterie, why are you crying? At the first
bright hint of spring the west wind will
bring back to you, rich with Bithynian
merchandise, your young and faithful

Gyges. Driven to Oricus by the east
wind and the Goat's insensate stars,
he passes the chilly nights waking
and weeps a myriad tears.

His fluttered hostess' maid
telling how sad Chloe sighs                         10
(alight with fires like yours),
tricksily tempts him a thousand ways.

She tells him how his wicked wife
by bearing false witness egged on
the gullible Proetus to plot an untimely death
for the too honest Bellerophon;

she speaks of Peleus, all but given over
to Tartarus for his abstinent flight
from Hippolyte; and subtly cites other
stories to teach him sin.                           20

In vain: for deafer than Icarus' cliffs
as yet he resists her temptations. But you
must beware lest Enipeus your neighbour
attract you more than he should

(I grant you no one else is so conspicuously good
at managing a horse on the Field of Mars,
and nobody swims as fast
as he can downstream in the Tiber).

Close up your house at dusk and don't
peep out when you hear in the street                    30
his cooing flute: and though he keeps calling
you hard-hearted, be stubborn.

# 8

## *Martiis caelebs*

You wonder what I, a bachelor, am about
on the Kalends of March; what is the meaning of
these flowers, this box of incense, these coals
    placed on fresh turf –

you, so versed in Greek and Latin customs? Well,
when I was nearly killed by that falling tree
I vowed to Bacchus a tasty dinner
    with a white goat.

Each year when this day comes round
I'll draw the well-sealed pitchy cork                    10
from a jar put up to bask in smoke when
    Tullus was consul.

So drink a hundred toasts, Maecenas,
to your friend's escape and let the lamps
burn on till dawn. Keep well away, all
    clamour and anger.

Let go your concern for the City.
Dacian Cotiso's column is crushed.
The perilous Parthians pitiably
    fight each other.                                    20

Our old friend the Cantabrian Spaniard
is tamed at last, a captive, in chains. Even
the Scythian, his bow unstrung, is considering
    flight from his plains.

Relax, be private, don't worry too much
about whether the people are suffering at all:
be glad to accept the here and now, and don't
    be serious.


# 9

## *Donec gratus eram*

'When I was dear to you
and no more favoured rival put his arms
    about your snowy neck,
I flourished then as bless'd as Persia's king.'

'When you burned for no one
more than for me and Lydia came before Chloe,
    Lydia's reputation
flourished as bright as Roman Ilia's name.'

'But Thracian Chloe rules
me now (a clever lyrist and skilled in seduct-            10
    ive modes), for whom I would
not fear to die if the Fates would let her live.'

'But Thurian Calais
kindles me now with a torch of mutual love,
    for whom I would die twice
if the Fates would agree to let my love live.'

'What if our love should come
again and Venus yoke her strays with bronze,
        blonde Chloe be jilted,
the door thrown open for disregarded Lydia?'          20

'Though he is as fair as a star
and you are as light as cork and bad-tempered
        as the Adriatic, I'd love
to live with you, with you would gladly die.'


# 10

## *Extremum Tanain*

If you drank from the distant Don, Lyce,
a savage's squaw, you would weep for me
stretched out in the bitter north wind
        before your hut.

You hear the creak of your gate, the groan
of the trees in your villa's elegant court
as Jupiter's pure divinity freezes
        the fallen snow?

Resign to Venus your graceless pride
lest the rope fall back from the whirling wheel.          10
No Tuscan fathered a girl as Penelope-
        frigid as you.

Though neither presents nor prayers
nor lovers' faces violet pale
nor husband hurt by a Pierian whore
        can sway you, spare

us suitors, o harder than oak
and softer than Moorish snakes.
I will not always tolerate sky, and
        rain, and doorstep.          20

## II

## *Mercuri — nam te*

Mercury, by whose magisterial teaching
Amphion's music moved the rocks;
and Tortoise-Shell skilled to resound
    to your seven strings,

once neither fluent nor liked, but now a friend
at rich men's tables and in the temples:
now sound the tones to which Lyde must lend
    her obstinate ear

(who like a three-year filly disports
herself on the open sward and shrinks from touch,    10
a stranger to marriage, as yet not ripe for
    an eager husband).

You have power to draw the tigers and woods
in your train, and stay the rushing brooks;
hell's janitor Cerberus succumbed
    to your enchantment,

though a hundred snakes defend
his raving heads, and foul breath
and bloody slaver flow
    from his triple maw.    20

Why, even Ixion and Tityos were forced
to smile; and the urn stood briefly dry
as you soothed with your pleasant song
    Danaus' daughters.

Let Lyde hear of those virgins' sin
and punishment, the liquid disappearing
through the base of the empty jar,
    the long-deferred fate

that awaits the guilty under Orcus.
Those monsters – what worse could they do? –                    30
those monstrous women put down their
  husbands with cold steel.

Just one of the many, a virgin
noble for ever, honoured the marriage torch
and was shiningly false to
  her perjured father.

'Get up!' she said to her youthful husband,
'get up! lest a long sleep come from where
you least suspect: frustrate my father
  and wicked sisters –                    40

alas! like a lioness making her kill,
each rends her own young bull: but I,
more gentle than them, will neither strike
  nor imprison you.

Let my father load me with cruel chains,
since I pity and spare my ill-used husband:
let him ship me to exile in the farthest parts
  of Numidia.

Go! wherever your feet and the breezes take you,
while Night and Venus assent. Go! while the signs                    50
are propitious, and carve on my tomb a sad
  commemoration.'


# 12

## *Miserarum est*

Frustrated women may neither give love play nor bathe
their cares in wine or else, dispirited, they fear
  the lash of Uncle's tongue.

Neobule, Venus's aerial boy upsets your wool,
your loom, your pious devotions to busy Minerva,
    the moment the brightness

that is Hebrus has bathed in Tiber his oiled shoulders –
a finer horseman he than Bellerophon himself;
    fist and foot, unbeaten;

canny to spear the stags stampeding in panicked herds     10
along the Campagna; and quick to intercept the boar
    routing in thickset brakes.

# 13

## *O fons Bandusiae*

Bandusian spring, more brilliant than glass,
worthy of flowers and classic wine,
tomorrow shall bring you a little goat
whose forehead bumpy with budding

horns prognosticates love and war –
in vain: the kidling of wanton herds
shall dye with his scarlet blood
your icy streams.

The terrible scorching Dog-Days cannot touch
the grateful chill you dispense     10
to roaming flocks and oxen
fatigued with the ploughshare.

You now shall become a famous spring
through my words for your dell in the rocks,
the ilex superimposed and
loquacious streams leaping down.

# 14

## *Herculis ritu*

Herculean Caesar, o people, who lately was said
to be earning the bays whose price is death,
returns once more to his household Gods
        as victor, from Spain.

Rejoicing in her paragon, sacrifice made
to the just Gods, let his consort come forward;
and our glittering premier's sister; and decked with
        suppliant head-bands,

the mothers of youths and virgins
recently spared. You boys and still                            10
unmarried girls, refrain from
        words of ill omen.

This day of days is festal indeed for me
and takes away black cares; I will fear
no insurrection nor violent death while
        Caesar keeps the world.

Go, find perfume boy, and garlands,
and a jar that remembers the Marsian troubles
(if any sherd has somehow evaded
        Spartacus' roving).                                    20

Bid witty Neaera make haste
to put up her hair and scent it with myrrh.
If that evil, grumbling janitor causes
        delay, ignore him.

My greying hair remits a litigious spirit
once eagerly looking for violent trouble:
I'd not have borne this in my fiery youth, when
        Plancus was consul.

## 15

### *Uxor pauperis Ibyci*

Impoverished Ibycus' wife,
keep within bounds your turpitudes
   and egregious doings:
ripening for interment, desist from

   playing the fool among maidens
and casting a cloud across brilliant stars.
   What suits Pholoe, Chloris,
does not quite suit you – fitter your daughter

   storm the homes of gallants,
a bacchante aroused by pulsing drums:         10
   love of Nothus makes her
cavort like a nannygoat in season.

   Fleeces shorn near Luceria,
not citharas or the crimson bloom
   of the rose or wine-jars
drunk to the dregs, become you, old.

## 16

### *Inclusam Danaen*

Brazen tower and oaken doors
and a surly watch of vigilant dogs
would have secured imprisoned Danae from
   nocturnal lechers

had Jove and Venus not mocked Acrisius,
the virgin's agitated guard: they knew
the way would be clear and safe when the
   God had cashed himself.

Gold loves to make its way through the midst
of attendants and break through rock, more potent     10
than thunderbolt's blow. For lucre the house of the
      Argive prophet fell

and sank in ruin; by bribes the Macedonian
split the gates of cities and undermined
all rival kings; percentages have ensnared
      fierce captains of ships.

Accumulating money creates the greed
for more. I was right to shrink from raising
my head to conspicuousness, Maecenas, you
      flower of knighthood.     20

The more a man denies himself, the more
he will get from the Gods: a deserter, I long to leave
the moneyed side, and seek the camp of those
      desiring nothing.

I am more the master of the wealth I spurn
than if, still poor amid my riches, I had
in my barns the produce of all that the busy
      Apulians plough.

A brook of pure water, few acres of timber,
and confident hope of harvest: my lot     30
is more bless'd than that of fertile
      Africa's bright lord.

Though Calabrian bees bring me no honey,
no wine matures for me in Laestrygonian
jars, no dense fleeces are growing for me
      in Gallic pastures:

yet irksome poverty does not come near,
nor if I wanted more would you refuse it.
By scanting my desires I shall the better
      augment my income     40

than by adding Alyattes' to Mygdon's realm,
the two to be contiguous. Who seeks much
lacks much. Bless'd is he to whom the Gods have
　　　given just enough.


# 17

## *Aeli vetusto*

Aelius, noble sprig of legendary Lamus
from whom, men say, the bygone Lamiae
and the line of their descendants took
their name through all recorded time;

you draw your blood from that founder,
that extensive tyrant said to have been
the first who held the walls of Formiae
and the Liris where it floods the Goddess

Marica's shores. Tomorrow, unless the ancient
crow, prophet of rain, deceive us, a tempest　　　　10
unleashed from the east shall strew the grove
with multitudinous leaves, the shore

with useless seaweed. Pile up dry wood
while you can: tomorrow, the tasks of your slaves
remitted, you shall comfort your soul
with unmixed wine and a piglet two months old.

# 18

## *Faune, Nympharum*

Faunus, lover of fugitive Nymphs,
gentle may you cross my bounds and sunny
meadows and bless the young of the flocks
    before you move on:

then at the full year's turn a kid shall fall
to you, largesse of wine shall brim the bowl
that's Venus' friend, and the ancient altar
    smoke with much incense.

The whole flock plays on the grassy plain
when the Nones of December come round;                    10
in the fields the parish and its idle cattle
    make their holiday;

the wolf now roams among fearless lambs;
for you the wild-wood sheds its leaves;
and the ditch-digger loves to tread his opponent
    earth in three-four time.


# 19

## *Quantum distet*

You relate how far removed in time
from Inachus was Codrus not afraid to die
    for his country; the genealogy of
Aeacus; and the war that was waged at sacred Troy:

but as to the price of a jar of Chian;
or who will light the fire to heat the water; and when
    and in whose house I may shut out
the Paelignian cold; you have nothing to say.

Boy, make haste. Here's to the moon!
Here's to midnight! Here's to Murena's augurship!  10
 In our bowls plain water is mixed
with three or nine stoups of wine according to taste.

 In a fine frenzy and in love
with the Muses' odd number, the poet asks for nine
 full stoups: fearing a fracas,
hand in hand with her naked sisters, Gratia

 prohibits a drop more than three.
It is good to run mad. But why has the piercing
 Berecyntian flute stopped playing?
Why do the pipe and lyre hang silent on the wall?  20

 I hate hands that hold
back. Scatter the roses. Make jealous Lycus
 hear our mind-blown din – and
his fair neighbour (she's too good for doddering Lycus).

 Ripe Rhode seeks you,
Telephus (with your gleaming mass of hair
 you are bright as the evening star):
slow fires of my love for Glycera scorify me.

# 20

## *Non vides quanto*

Do you not see, Pyrrhus, at what grave personal risk
you touch the cub of this North African lion-
ess? Soon, a cowardly thief, you will
  shun a hard fight

when, seeking her glamorous Nearchus,
she goes through the crowd of obstructive youths.
A heroic duel must decide which one of you two
  shall have the prey.

Meanwhile, as you count swift arrows out
and she makes sharp her appalling teeth,          10
the referee (and prize) of the match is said to
          trample the palm

with his naked feet and cool in the gentle breeze
his shoulders overspread with perfumed locks –
just like Nireus or the boy shanghai'd from
          many-springed Ida.


# 21

## *O nata mecum*

O faithful jar that was born
like me when Manlius was consul,
whether you bring complaints, or jokes,
or insensate quarrels and love, or easy sleep,

for whatever end was gathered the Massic
you keep, fit to be served on some
auspicious day, come down, since Corvinus
requires a maturer wine.

Steeped though he is in Socratic
dialogues, he's not uncouth, will not neglect you.          10
It is reported that even Cato's
old-time morals grew often warm in wine.

You apply a gentle compulsion to wits
that are otherwise dull; you and jesting
Bacchus uncover wise men's
preoccupations and secret counsels;

you bring back hope to despairing minds;
add spirit and strength to the poor,
who after you tremble neither at the crowns
of angry kings nor at the soldiery's weapons.          20

Bacchus and Venus, if it please
her to come, and the Graces, slow to break
their bond, and burning lamps attend you
till returning Phoebus puts the stars to flight.

## 22

### *Montium custos*

Guardian of hills and groves; Virgin
who, called for three times, attends to young
women in labour and saves them from death;
　　　three-formed Goddess;

yours be the pine that overtops my house:
then as each year passes by may I gladly kill
a young boar practising sidelong thrusts and
　　　offer his blood.

## 23

### *Caelo supinas*

If you lift your upturned palms to the sky
at each new moon, my rustic Phidyle,
and appease the Lares with incense,
fresh fruit and a greedy pig,

then your fecund vines shall not feel
the blighting south wind, nor cornfields
barren mould, nor sweet young stock
hard times in apple-bearing autumn.

For the dedicated victim that grazes now
on snowy Algidus beneath the ilex and oak                    10
or else grows fat on Alban grass
shall dye from its neck

the hatchets of the priests. But you have
no need for great carnage: you can assuage
your small Gods with rosemary crowns
and delicate myrtle garlands.

If the hands that touch the altar be pure
(though lacking the unction of costly blood),
they can soothe estranged Penates
with sacred meal and sputtering salt.                    20

# 24

## *Intactis opulentior*

    Richer than the intact
Arabian exchequer and the Indies' store,
      you fill our Tuscan land
and the common sea with your building-works:

    yet if dire Necessity fix
her adamant nails in your rooftop,
      your soul shall not escape
from terror nor your neck from death's noose.

    The Scythian tribes of the plains,
whose nomad homes are on waggons, and stiff-                    10
      necked Getae live better,
for whom unnumbered acres make communal

    harvests under Ceres.
Each brave works a year on the land:
      his service remitted,
a successor continues by equal rota.

There stepmothers behave
rationally to orphaned daughters,
   no women rule by dowry
and wives do not trust in some sleek adulterer.      20

The dower of their families is
manliness and chastity which, surely
   contracted, avoids other men:
sin is forbidden and its price is death.

Whoever may wish to root out
seditious killings and internecine madness,
   if he aspire to be styled
on monuments *Father of Cities*, oh let him dare

to bridle unbroken licence
and his fame will shine down through posterity.     30
   Alas, how we hate sound goodness:
yet once it is out of sight, we enviously seek it.

What is the point of complaint
if guilt is not felled by the judge's sentence?
   What help are empty laws
without morals, if no place on earth

(in the burning tropics
or enduring snows of the Arctic marches)
   drives out merchants,
and seasoned sailors can overcome      40

the stormy seas; if poverty,
deemed a disgrace, commands us to do
   and allow what we will,
and abandons arduous Virtue's path?

Let us bring to the Capitol
(to which applause, approval's hubbub, calls)
   or throw in the nearest sea
if we truly repent of our crimes

our gems and jewels, useless gold,
the very substance of our gross misfortune.          50
     The roots of unnatural greed
must be excised and excessively tender

     minds must be shaped
to austerer studies. No freeborn boy
     these days can sit a horse,
and hunting scares him. He is taught instead to play

     either with a Greek hoop
or at dice-games banned by feeble laws –
     as his father perjures himself
to defraud his partner and even his guests,          60

     and puts by money
for his worthless heir. His shameful riches
     certainly grow – and yet
some little something, some trifle, is always lacking.


# 25

## *Quo me, Bacche, rapis*

Bacchus, where will you carry me
full of you? My spirit renewed, what groves and grottoes
     am I driven into? In what ravine
shall I now be heard planning to set among the stars

     and in Jove's council
peerless Caesar's immortal glory?
     I tell of a wonder as yet
untold by other lips. Just as in the mountains

     the insomniac Dionysian stands rapt
at the prospect of Hebrus and snow-gleaming Thrace          10
     and Rhodope trodden
by barbarous feet, just so is it my

pleasure to wonder
at unregarded banks and groves
    deserted. O master of the Naiads
and Bacchanalians strong to uproot the princely ash,

I shall utter nothing
insignificant, lowly or not immortal. Sweet the risk,
    Lenaean, to follow the God,
crowning one's brows with sprouting vine leaves.          20


# 26

## *Vixi puellis nuper*

In the past I kept myself fit
for girls and campaigned with some glory:
now this wall that guards the left
of sea-born Venus shall bear

my arms and defunctive lyre.
Place here, and here, the burning
torches, the levers and axes
that menaced opposing doors.

O Goddess, who keeps bless'd Cyprus
and Memphis free from snow, o queen,          10
with your lifted whip please flick
conceited Chloe just once.

# 27

## *Impios parrae*

May these omens indict the wicked:
a hooting owl, a pregnant bitch, a grey
wolf loping down from Lanuvium,
    a whelping vixen.

A snake shall dart across their path
and break their journey by making
the ponies stampede. I am an
    augur who favours

the people I care for: for you
I waken at sunrise the croaking raven         10
before he returns to the stagnant marsh
    to prophesy rain.

Good luck, my Galatea, may be wherever
you go. Do not forget me. May no wood-
pecker on the left or rambling crow
    forbid your going.

But you see the welter in which
Orion, sinking, rages. I know too well
what the black gulf of the Adriatic and
    clear north wind can do.         20

I would wish on our enemies' children
and wives the blind thrust of that rising wind,
the roars of the darkling sea, the beaches
    vibrating with shock.

So bold Europa entrusted her snowy flanks
to the treacherous bull – and soon turned pale
at the perils of the sea, the deep
    alive with monsters.

Lately in the meadows a student of flowers,
a weaver of garlands due to the Nymphs,                    30
now she saw in the glimmering night nothing
    but the stars and waves.

As soon as she landed in Crete, mighty
with its hundred towns, 'Father!' she cried,
'oh name of daughter and duty forsaken!
    oh whence and whither

am I come in my frenzy? One death
is too light for a virgin's shame. Do I lament
a horrid fact, or am I guiltless and does
    some phantom mock me,                              40

that flying vaguely through the ivory gate
brings but a dream? Was it better
to journey amid the long waves, or
    to pluck fresh flowers?

If that loathsome bullock were delivered
to my anger, I would try to stab with a sword
and break the horns of the monster
    I recently loved.

Shameless, I deserted my household Gods;
shameless, I keep Orcus waiting. If any God                50
hear my words, oh let me wander
    nude among lions!

Before repulsive wasting can attack
my comely cheeks, before the life-blood
has drained from the tender prey, I will feed my
    beauty to tigers!

"Worthless Europa," I hear my father say,
"why so long about dying? You could hang
yourself on this tree – luckily your sash
    is still at your waist.                             60

Or if the cliffs and deadly sharp rocks
attract you, go ahead, entrust yourself
to the hurrying gale – unless you would rather
    be handed over,

a concubine-princess, to card the wool for some
barbarian queen!" ' Venus stood watching
her plaint with a tricksy smile, and her son,
    with his bow unstrung.

When she had gloated enough, 'Curb
your tantrums and hot resentment,' she said,      70
'when the detested bull brings you his
    horns to be broken.

Know you are wife to invincible Jove.
Stop sobbing, and learn to bear yourself
as befits your destiny: half the world
    shall be named for you.'

# 28

## *Festo quid potius die*

What better way to honour
Neptune's feast-day? Bring out the hidden
    Caecuban, Lyde, quick,
let us set a siege against wisdom's fortress.

You see that noon is past
and yet, as though the fleeting day stood still,
    you put off fetching from the pantry
the jar that survives from Bibulus' year as consul.

Let's sing by turns: first I
of Neptune and the Nereids' sea-green hair:      10
    then take your curving lyre
and respond with Latona; swift Cynthia's darts;

and as your finale, praise her
who keeps the shining Cyclades, and Cnidos, and visits
    Paphos with her harnessed swans:
and Night shall be sung in a congruous hymn.


# 29

## *Tyrrhena regum progenies*

Maecenas, descendant of Etruscan kings, for you
a jar of smooth wine as yet untilted
    and roses in bloom and balsam
crushed out for your hair have long stood ready

at my estate. Avoid all hindrance:
do not for ever contemplate
    well-watered Tibur, Aefula's sloping meadows,
the parricide Telegonus' ridge.

Abandon wearisome plenty, the pile
that approaches the soaring clouds;            10
    leave wondering at the smoke,
the money, the din of wealthy Rome.

A change is usually pleasant:
a wholesome meal in a poor man's modest home
    with no fine purple fabrics
can smooth the rich man's troubled brow.

Already Andromeda's bright father
declares his hidden fire; already Procyon rages,
    and the star of Leo raves, as the sun
brings back the days of drought;            20

already the shepherd with his listless flock
seeks out the shade, the brook, and shaggy
    Silvanus' thickets; and the silent bank
lacks any wandering breeze.

You worry as to what conditions best befit
the State; concerned for the City, you fear
what the Seres may do next, or Bactra
(once ruled by Cyrus), or the dissident Don.

Wisely the God enwraps in fuliginous night
the future's outcome, and laughs                        30
if mortals are anxious beyond
mortality's bound. Take care to deal equably

with what is present. The rest is borne along
like a river, now gliding peacefully down
within its bed to the Tuscan
sea; now rolling together in one

gouged boulders, uprooted trees, and flocks,
and homes, with echoes resounding back
from the hills and adjacent woods –
the turbulent flash-flood convulses                      40

quiet streams. A happy life and mastery
over himself shall be his who daily
can say: 'I have lived: tomorrow the Father
may fill the vault with dark clouds

or brilliant sunlight, but he will not render
the past invalid, will not re-shape
and make undone whatever
the fleeting hour has brought.'

Pleased with her cruel dealings, resolved
to play her high-handed game, Fortune               50
shuffles her doubtful benefits,
benign now to me, but now to some other.

I praise her as long as she stays: if she spreads
her swift wings, I renounce her gifts
and clad in my manhood pay court to honest
Poverty, though she brings no dowry.

It is not my way, when the mast is groaning
with southerly squalls, to rush
into craven prayer and bargain with vows
in case my Cyprian and Tyrian wares                    60

should add to the wealth of the gaping sea:
then Pollux, his twin, and the breeze
shall bring me safe in my two-oared dinghy
through this Aegean tumult.


# 30

## *Exegi monumentum*

I have achieved a monument more lasting
than bronze, and loftier than the pyramids of kings,
which neither gnawing rain nor blustering wind
may destroy, nor innumerable series of years,
nor the passage of ages. I shall not wholly die,
a large part of me will escape Libitina:
while Pontiff and Vestal shall climb the Capitol Hill,
I shall be renewed and flourish in further praise.
Where churning Aufidus resounds, where Daunus
poor in water governed his rustic people,                    10
I shall be spoken of as one who was princely
though of humble birth, the first to have brought
Greek song into Latin numbers. Take hard-won pride
in your success, Melpomene, and willingly
wreathe my hair with Apollo's laurel.

# CENTENNIAL
# HYMN

# Phoebe silvarumque

Phoebus, bright glory of heaven,
Diana, queen of the forests, o worshipped
and ever to be so, grant what we pray
          at this sacred time

when the Sibyl's verses have ordered
chosen virgins and virtuous boys
to sing a hymn to the Gods who
          love the Seven Hills.

Kind Sun, who in your shining chariot reveal
and then conceal the day, reborn another and yet          10
the same, may you view nothing greater than
          the City of Rome.


Ilithyia, gently bringing on birth
at the proper time, whether you more approve
the name Lucina or Genitalis,
          protect our mothers.

Goddess, rear our young and prosper
the Senate's edicts on wedlock, that the new
law on the marriage of women produce
          abundant children,                                          20

and the sure cycle of eleven decades
bring round once more the singing and games
thronged thrice by broad day and thrice
          in the pleasant night.


And you veracious Fates, may the outcome
of events confirm what has been pronounced,
and link our happy destinies with those
          already performed.

Let the earth, so fertile in crops and cattle,
deck Ceres with a wheaten wreath:                          30
may the wholesome breezes and rains of Jove
    sustain the new-born.

Calm and peaceful, your bow laid aside,
Apollo, hear our suppliant boys;
and Luna, twin-horned queen of
    the stars, hear our girls.


If Rome is your work and from Ilium
the bands that gained the Tuscan shore (the remnant
commanded to change their homes and city in an
    auspicious process,                          40

for whom righteous Aeneas, his country's survivor,
unharmed through burning Troy secured
the way to freedom, destined to provide more
    than was left behind),

Gods! give proven morals to our ductile youth,
Gods! give rest to our sober elders,
give profit, progeny and every honour
    to Romulus' race.


Whatever he of Anchises' and Venus' pure blood
(a warrior heretofore, now lenient to the fallen          50
foe) entreats of you with white bulls,
    grant him his prayers.

Now the Parthian fears the Alban axes,
the forces mighty by sea and land;
now Scythians and Indians, lately so proud,
    await our answer.

Now Faith, and Peace, and Honour,
and pristine Modesty, and Manhood neglected,
dare to return, and blessèd Plenty appears
    with her laden horn.                          60

Phoebus, adorned with his shining bow,
a prophet, companion of the nine Muses,
who with his healing art relieves the
    body's weary limbs,

if he looks with favour on the Palatine altars,
prolongs the Roman State and Latium's
affluence through cycles ever new and
    ages ever better.

Diana, who keeps the Aventine
and Algidus, heeds the prayers of         70
the Fifteen Men and lends a friendly ear
    to the children's vows.


The chorus trained to sing the praises
of Phoebus and Diana, we carry home the good
and steadfast hope that Jove and all the Gods
    approve these wishes.

# ODES

## BOOK IV

# I

## *Intermissa, Venus*

Then is it war again, Venus,
after so long a truce? Mercy, mercy, please.
   I am not as I was in the reign
of my dear Cinara. Desist, fierce mother

   of pretty Cupids;
do not bend my inflexible five decades
   to your tender command; go away –
attend to the fluent prayers of younger men.

   Carousal would be
more timely in Paulus Maximus' house:                    10
   take your silver swans to him
if you seek a suitable liver to inflame.

Both high-born and handsome,
not silent on behalf of the anxious defendant,
   this youth has a hundred arts
to advance your standards far and wide:

   and when he has mocked
and surpassed some rival's lavish gifts,
   Paulus will erect your statue
under citrus beams by the Alban lake.                     20

   There you shall snuff
much incense; and a choir concerted with lyres
   and Berecyntian flutes,
and recorders too, shall strive to attract you:

   there twice a day youths
and tender girls praising your godhead
   shall pace with gleaming feet
in the triple step of the Salian dance.

But me – neither woman, boy,
nor credulous hope of sharing souls,                                    30
    nor contests in wine,
nor garlands about my hair, can move me now.

Then why, my Ligurinus, why
these unaccustomed tears on my cheeks?
   ·Why does my eloquent tongue
ineptly fall silent among the words?

Each night in my dreams
I hold you captive, or else pursue
    your obdurate flight
across the Field of Mars, through swirling water.                       40

# 2

## *Pindarum quisquis*

Whoever attempts to emulate Pindar, Julus,
depends from wings that are fastened with wax
by Daedalian art and shall give his name
    to some glassy sea.

As a river swollen by the rains above its usual
banks rushes down from the mountain,
so does Pindar surge and his deep
    voice rushes on,

commanding the prize of Apollo's bays
whether he rolls new words along in audacious                           10
dithyrambs and is carried by numbers
    freed from convention;

or tells of Gods or kings of the blood
of Gods, through whom the Centaurs in just
execution died, and died the fire of
    the daunting Chimaera;

whether he speaks of those boxers
and charioteers whom Elean palms bring
God-like home (an honour more signal than
    a hundred statues);                                           20

or laments the young hero torn from his
weeping bride, and extols to the stars (and grudges
to Orcus' darkness) his strength, his spirit,
    his golden virtue.

A mighty wind lifts the swan of Dirce,
Antonius, whenever he strives for some high tract
of clouds; but I, very much in the manner
    of a Matine bee

laboriously harvesting thyme
from numerous groves and the banks of many-                   30
streamed Tibur, inconspicuously accrete
    my intricate verses.

A maker of larger mettle, you shall celebrate
Caesar deservèdly, fittingly wreathed,
dragging the wild Sygambri along
    the Sacred Way;

than whom the Fates and good Gods have given
and shall give the world nothing greater or better,
though time itself ran back to the
    pristine age of gold.                                    40

You shall celebrate festive days
and the City's games that mark the return
of brave Augustus and the Forum free
    from litigation.

And then, if I can tell something worth
the hearing, the better part of my voice shall join
and bless'd in Caesar I'll sing: 'O beauteous day,
    o worthy of praise!'

And as you take the lead, the State entire
shall cry 'Hail Triumph!' and again 'Hail Triumph!'        50
And plenteous incense shall be offered up
        to the kindly Gods.

Ten bulls and as many cows shall acquit
your vow: a tender calf mine,
which has left its mother and attained its youth
        amid lush pastures,

its brow resembling the crescent curve
of the new moon at its third rising,
snowy white where it bears that mark,
        all else pure ochre.        60

# 3

## *Quem tu, Melpomene*

He whom once you, Melpomene,
have looked on at his birth with peaceful eyes,
        shall not by Isthmian strife
become a famous boxer, and no impetuous stallion

        shall draw him to victory in
his Achaean chariot, nor shall martial deeds
        display him to the Capitol,
an officer decked with a Delian wreath, for crushing

        the vengeful threats of kings;
but the waters that flow past fertile Tibur        10
        and the groves' dense manes
shall build him a reputation for Aeolian song.

        The children of Rome, the queen
of cities, consider me worthy to rank among
        the choir of the poets whom
they love, and already envy's teeth bite less.

Pierian virgin who governs
the golden tones of the tortoise-shell lyre,
    you that could give, should
you want, the voices of swans to dumb fish,                    20

        this is the sum of your gifts:
that I am pointed out by passers-by as an adept
        of the Roman lyre; and if
I please, I please because inspired by you.


# 4

## *Qualem ministrum*

As the winged bearer of lightning,
to whom the king of the Gods granted sway
over the birds of the air, having found him loyal
in the case of longhaired Ganymede;

whom, ignorant of difficulties, youth
and hereditary liveliness thrust
from the eyrie; whom, fearful,
rain-clouds removed, the vernal gales

teach unaccustomed efforts; who soon
plummets down in joyous attack on the
sheep-fold; whose love of feasting and fighting
drives him down against struggling snakes:

as a lion just weaned from his tawny
mother's rich milk, by whose
young teeth shall perish
a she-goat intent on rich pasture:

such was Drusus when the Vindelici saw
his advance beneath the Rhaetian Alps.
(Whence was derived the custom
that for all time has equipped them with                       20

the Amazonian axe, I have omitted to inquire,
nor is it good to know all.) Their long
and widely victorious hordes
were defeated by that young tactician;

were made to feel what intellect, what inborn talent
correctly raised beneath an auspicious roof,
could do, and Augustus' paternal purpose
toward the youthful Neros.

Brave men are born to the brave and good;
their fathers' sternness appears in bulls                          30
and stallions; fierce eagles
beget no pacific doves.

But nurture increases native powers, development
of righteousness strengthens the heart:
whenever character has been unmade,
weakness has dirtied things born sound.

What you owe to the Neros, Rome,
witness the river Metaurus and Hasdrubal
overthrown and the fair day
darkness was driven from Latium –                                 40

the first to smile with victory's reward
since the dire Carthaginian rode
through Italy's towns like fire through pines
or Eurus across the Sicilian waves.

Thereafter the youth of Rome grew strong
(its efforts ever successful) and set upright
its Gods in the shrines laid waste
by sacrilegious devastation.

At last perfidious Hannibal said:
'Like deer, the prey of ravening wolves,                          50
we follow those it were a signal
triumph to confuse and evade.

The race, so strong from Ilium's burning,
which brought its sacred idols, its sons
and agèd fathers through tossing
Tuscan seas to Ausonian towns,

an ilex lopped by hard axes amid
Algidus' dense umbrageous greenery,
by loss and by slaughter draws its strength
and spirit from the iron sword itself.                    60

No stronger grew the flesh-hacked Hydra against
Alcides grieving to think of defeat;
and neither Colchis nor Cadmus' Thebes
reared up so great a prodigy.

Drown it in the deeps, it emerges more fair:
wrestle, and to great applause it will throw
a champion as yet unbeaten
and bring off fights for wives to retail.

I may send no more proud messengers
to Carthage: fallen, fallen all our hope                  70
and the fortunes of our name
since Hasdrubal's disaster.

There is nothing that Claudian force
may not perform, which Jupiter's kind
divinity defends, which shrewd counsels
deliver from the crises of war.'

# 5

## *Divis orte bonis*

Sprung from the Gods, first guardian of the race
of Romulus, already your absence is too long:
since you promised the sacred council
of the Senate an early return, return.

Give back the light, dear leader, to your country:
for when, like spring, your face
has flashed upon the people, more pleasant
runs the day and the sun shines brighter.

As with vows, with omens and with prayers
a mother calls for more than a year her son                    10
whom Notus with jealous bluster detains
lingering far from his sweet home

across the stretches of Carpathian sea,
nor turns her face from the curving bay:
so, smitten with loyal love,
his fatherland yearns for Caesar.

For when he's here the ox in safety roams
the pasture and Ceres and kind Prosperity
feed the farmland and sailors glide across
peaceful seas; good faith fears rightful blame;          20

no lewdness pollutes the chaste home;
custom and law cast out spotted sin; mothers
are praised for their children's family likeness;
punishment presses close behind guilt.

Who would fear the Parthians, who the icy
Scythian, who the brood that bristling Germany
bears, with Caesar unharmed? And who
would mind the war with feral Spain?

Each man passes the day on his own hillside,
marrying his vines to lonely trees;                            30
thence he gladly returns to his wine, and at
the second course invokes your godhead:

he worships you with many prayers
and pure wine poured from bowls, and mingles
your power with his household Gods, like the Greek
who remembers Castor and mighty Alcides.

'Dear leader, grant long holidays
to Italy!' we say dry-mouthed
at break of day, and say again having drunk
when the sun is beneath the ocean.                            40

# 6

## *Dive, quem proles*

God, whom Niobe's children and the robber
Tityos found to punish bombast, and when
he was nearly the victor of lofty Troy,
    Phthian Achilles

(greater than the rest but still no match for you,
although the warrior son of Sea-goddess Thetis;
who shook the Dardanian towers with his
    appalling lance;

who, like some pine-tree smitten with biting
iron or cypress uprooted by the east wind,        10
fell sprawling flat and laid his head
    in the Trojan dust;

who did not hide in the horse, that spurious
offering to Minerva, to deceive the Trojans
keeping holiday and Priam's court rejoicing
    in the dances,

but openly harsh to his captives – alas, alas,
the sin – would sooner have burned in Argive fires
the innocent children, even the baby concealed
    in his mother's womb,       20

had not the Father of the Gods, won over
by your and by pleasant Venus' pleas, vowed as
Aeneas' wierd that with better auspices other
    walls would be raised):

lyrist, teacher of clear-voiced Thalia,
Phoebus, who wash your hair in Xanthus river,
smooth-cheeked Agyieus, protect the splendour
    of the Daunian Muse.

Phoebus gave me my inspiration, Phoebus
my skill in song and the name of poet.                    30
First among virgins and young men born of
    illustrious blood,

wards of the Delian Goddess whose bow
stops dead the stags and fleeing lynxes,
observe the Lesbian metre and
    beat of my thumb,

as you duly sing to Latona's son,
duly to Nightshining's waxing torch,
who ripens the crops and swiftly revolves
    the pressing months.                               40

Married, you'll say: 'When the festal Centennial
days came round, I joined in the hymn that heartens
the Gods, for I was trained in the measures of
    the poet Horace.'

# 7

## *Diffugere nives*

Snows are dissolved and grass returns to the meadows
    and foliage to trees;
Earth suffers her changes and diminishing rivers run
    between their banks;

Gratia with her Nymphs and twin sisters dares,
    naked, to lead the dance.
The year and the hour that snatch our day warn us not
    to hope for eternal life.

Frosts melt for Zephyr; the summer tramples
    the spring but will die                            10
when autumn pours out harvest; and soon the numb
    short days recur.

Swift moons, moreover, recoup their celestial losses:
    when we have fallen and joined
our father Aeneas and opulent Tullus and Ancus,
    we are dust and shadow.

Who knows whether the high Gods will add more tomorrows
    to the sum of todays?
Devote the whole sheaf to your own sweet will and thwart
    the avid hands of your heir.                    20

When once you have perished and Minos has passed
    his royal verdict,
neither race, Torquatus, nor eloquence, nor righteous
    deeds shall restore you:

for even Diana cannot free her celibate Hippolytus
    from the underworld's murk;
nor can Theseus prevail to break the Lethean bonds
    of his dear Pirithous.

# 8

## *Donarem pateras*

I would give generously to my intimates,
Censorinus, bowls and charming bronzes,
I would give tripods, the prizes of athletic
Greeks, nor would you carry off the least
of my presents, were I but rich, of course,
in works Parrhasius made, or Scopas,
the one in liquid colours, the other in stone,
skilled to present now a man, now a God.
But I have no such means, nor does your spirit
or condition stand in want of such luxuries.                    10
You revel in poems, and poems I can give,
and name the value of such tributes.
Not marble incised with public records,

whereby breath and life return to good commanders
who are gone, nor Hannibal's swift retreat,
his threats rebounding back upon himself,
nor the burning of sacrilegious Carthage, declare
more shiningly the fame of him who returned
having won his name from Africa's subjection,
than do the Calabrian Muses: and you would get                    20
no reward if parchment were silent on what
you have done, and done well. What were the son
of Ilia and Mars if envious taciturnity
had obstructed the path of Romulus' deserts?
The powers, good-will and speech of potent poets
redeem Aeacus from the waves of Styx,
and waft him to the Islands of the Bless'd.
The Muse forbids the praiseworthy man to die,
the Muse bestows heaven. Thus strenuous
Hercules shared the hoped-for feasts of Jove,                    30
the Tyndarides (shining constellation)
snatch shattered craft from the sea's deep maw,
and Bacchus, his temples decked with vine-shoots,
brings vows to happy consummations.


# 9

## *Ne forte credas*

Do not believe the words will perish
which I, born by sounding Aufidus,
enounce and blend with plucked strings
by skills hitherto unpublished:

though Homer keeps the seat of honour,
yet the Muses of Pindar, of Ceos,
of menacing Alcaeus, and of stately
Stesichorus are not lost;

nor have the ages deleted the trifles Anacreon
cheerfully sang; the love of the Aeolian                    10
girl still lives, and the ardours
committed to her lyre.

Not only Spartan Helen was inflamed
and wondered at an adulterer's
coiffure, gold-tissued robes,
and regal pomp and satellites;

nor was Teucer the first to aim the shaft
from Cretan bow; Troy was besieged
more than once; not mighty
Idomeneus and Sthenelus alone fought                    20

battles the Muses might sing; nor was
doughty Hector nor quick Deiphobus
the first to accept hard knocks
for his modest wife and his children.

Many heroes lived before Agamemnon,
but all are oppressed in unending night,
unwept, unknown, because they lack
a dedicated poet.

In the tomb, courage differs little
from disgrace. In my books,                    30
I will not tacitly omit to praise you,
Lollius, nor will I suffer

envious oblivion to graze on your many
exploits. You have a mind well versed
in managing affairs, upright both
in favourable and in doubtful times,

punishing greedy fraud, holding aloof
from money that draws all things to itself,
consul not for a single year
but whenever, a good and faithful judge,                    40

you prefer honesty to expediency,
reject with averted face the bribes of
the guilty, and deploy your victorious army
against the obstructing hosts.

We could not rightly call bless'd the man
who possesses much: more properly he fills
that designation who has learned to use
wisely the gifts of the Gods,

to endure harsh poverty and fear
dishonour worse than death –                    50
the man who is not afraid to perish
for his dear friends or his country.


# 10

## *O crudelis adhuc*

When stubble comes unlooked-for upon your pride,
o cruel still and potent with Venus's gifts;
those curls that flounce on your shoulders fall;
your complexion as fine as the pinkest rose,
Ligurinus, transform to a growth of beard:
'Oh!' you'll say when your mirror shows the change,
'why was I not as a child of my present mind,
or why can't pristine cheeks assist my heart?'

# 11

## *Est mihi nonum*

I have a full jar of Alban wine more than nine
years old; there is in my garden, Phyllis,
parsley for twining in crowns; there is
    ivy in plenty

to bind back your hair so you dazzle;
the villa smiles with silver; the altar wreathed in
sacred foliage longs for the sprinkled blood of
    a sacrificed lamb;

the household's full muster makes haste, hither
and thither it hurries, girls mingled with boys;    10
the flickering flames rotate the
    sooty smoke in whorls.

I should explain the revels to which
you are invited: they are to mark
the Ides, the day that sunders April, the month
    of sea-born Venus –

by rights a religious day to me,
more sacred almost than my own birthday,
for from this dawn my own Maecenas reckons
    his on-going years.    20

Young Telephus, your fancy (but above
your station), a rich and lickerish girl
has captured, and keeps him hobbled
    in grateful shackles.

Phaethon scorched warns over-ambitious
hope, and Pegasus weighed down
by terrestrial Bellerophon provides
    an urgent example –

always to aim for what is fitting, and deeming
it sin to hope for what is not allowed,                    30
to shun a disparate match. Then come,
          you last of my loves

(hereafter I shall wax warm for no
woman), study measures your love-requiring
voice may repeat: melancholy may be
          diminished by song.


# 12

## *Iam veris comites*

Already the breath of Thrace, the attendant
of spring, is calming the sea and propelling sails,
meadows no longer are frozen, nor do
the rivers roar, turgid with winter's snow.

The unhappy swallow builds her nest,
keening and weeping for Itys, sempiternal shame
of Cecrops' house, because she avenged
too cruelly the barbarous lust of kings.

In the lush grass the fat sheep's
guardians play songs on their pipes                       10
and delight the God to whom are dear
Arcadia's flocks and umbrageous hills.

Virgilius, the season has brought us drought:
if you (a protégé of noble youths) wish truly
to sample a wine that was pressed at Cales,
you must earn your cup with nard.

A little pot of nard elicits a jar
stored now in some Sulpician warehouse,
sufficiently large to give new hope, and efficacious
to wash away your bitter cares.                           20

If you are eager for such relief, come quickly
with your fee: if you come empty-handed
I don't envisage you damping your thirst
at my table – for I am no fat squire.

Set aside delay and thought of gain
and mindful of darkness burning mix
brief sottishness with wisdom while you may:
it is sweet to play the clown upon occasion.

# 13

## *Audivere, Lyce*

The Gods have heard my prayer, Lyce,
Lyce, the Gods have heard: you are old,
and yet you want to seem lovely
and sportive, and you drink,

and drunk you solicit indifferent Cupid
with a quavering song. Cupid, however,
keeps watch and flourishes in clever
musical Chia's fair cheeks.

Rude, he won't break his flight for sapless
oaks and avoids you – for yellow teeth                    10
and wrinkles and the snow
on your head pollute you.

Nor glistening Coan silk nor precious
gems can bring you back the days
that transient time has shut away
in superseded calendars.

Alas, where has Venus fled, and where
complexion and graceful carriage – oh where
is she, Cinara's happy successor,
that she who breathed desire,                             20

whose noted form and charming skills
usurped me from myself? To Cinara
the Fates allowed few years,
but Lyce shall be long

preserved, an agèd crow,
that burning young men may study
(not without much laughter)
the torch collapsed in ashes.

# 14

## *Quae cura patrum*

What adequate honours and emoluments
have the Senate and Quirites
to perpetuate through the ages by inscriptions
and commemorations your perfected

manhood, Augustus, o mightiest of generals
wherever the sun illumines inhabitable regions,
whose capability in war the Vindelici
(hitherto exempt from Roman law)

have lately learned? For with your troops
fierce Drusus, in more than equal retribution,                10
hurled down the Genauni (implacable tribe)
and the swift Breuni together with

their strongholds perched on the dizzy Alps.
Soon the older Nero joined stern battle
and under happy auspices
overcame the savage Rhaetians,

a fine sight in martial combat
for the chaos he made in havocking
those resolved to die unconquered:
almost as, when the Pleiades                                  20

pierce the clouds, the south wind frets
the indomitable waves, so he was eager
to harass the enemy host and drive
his neighing horse through the midst of fire.

As bullish Aufidus rolls on,
flowing by the realms of Apulian Daunus,
and rages and threatens the cultivated fields
with horrifying floods,

so with an all-out charge Claudius
destroyed the barbarians' iron-clad columns:                   30
mowing down van and rear, suffering
no set-backs, the victor strewed the ground,

prevailing by your troops, your plan, and by
your Gods. And on the very date
when suppliant Alexandria threw open
her harbours and vacated palace,

propitious Fortune thrice five years later
conferred on you a happy end to the war,
bestowing fame and well-sought glory
for what was done in enacting your commands.                   40

The Cantabrian (never before civilized),
the Mede, the Indian and the fugitive Scythian
marvel at you, o powerful shield
of Italy and her mistress Rome.

The Nile who hides the sources of
his streams, the Danube, the swirling Tigris,
the monster-infested ocean
that roars round far-flung Britain,

and Gaul not daunted by death, and the harsh
land of Spain, all harken to you: to you                       50
the slaughter-enjoying Sygambri
do homage and lay down their arms.

# 15

## *Phoebus volentem*

Phoebus cut short with his lyre my wish
to tell of battles and cities sacked,
lest I should set my little sails
to an epic wind. Augustus, your reign

has brought rich harvests and fertile fields,
restores to Roman Jove our standards torn
from insolent Parthian porches,
and free from warfare preserves

the Arcade of Janus closed, and by the bridle
drags back rank-breaking runaway licence                    10
to propriety, and cancels guilt,
and calls back ancient arts

whereby the Latin name and Roman power
have arisen and the majesty of Empire
extends from the couch of Hesper
to the rising of the sun.

While Augustus guards our affairs,
nor civil strife nor force shall drive out peace,
nor shall sword-forging wrath
beset any wretched city.                                    20

Drinkers from the deep Danube shall not break
the Julian edicts, nor the Getae,
nor the Seres or treacherous Parthians,
nor any indigenous to the Don.

And we, on festal and working days,
amid the gifts of cheerful Bacchus,
our wives and children about us,
having prayed to the Gods in due form,

shall like our forefathers sing
(to Lydian pipes) heroes who died well,                    30
and Troy, and Anchises, and all
the progeny of kindly Venus.

# APPENDIX

## *Suetonius*

## *The Life of Horace*

*This brief 'life' is attached to some of the early MSS of Horace and is generally accepted as an abbreviated transcription of the* Vita Horatii *which Suetonius had included in the section on poets in his* Lives of Illustrious Men. *Its main interest lies in the light it throws on the relations between Horace and Augustus through the letters quoted. Some of Augustus' voluminous correspondence had been published but, as personal secretary to the emperor Hadrian and Head of the Imperial Chancery, Suetonius would have had access to unpublished letters of past emperors.*

Quintus Horatius Flaccus was born in Venusia, the son of a freedman, as he says himself, who was an auctioneer's assistant (though it is popularly believed that he was a seller of salt fish on the strength of someone's taunt to Horace during a quarrel – 'How often I've seen your father wipe his nose on his arm!'). In the fighting at Philippi he served as military tribune when called upon by the leader Marcus Brutus, and after his side was defeated he was pardoned and obtained the position of clerk to the quaestors. He was then introduced to Maecenas and subsequently to Augustus, and held high place amongst the friends of both. How dearly Maecenas loved him is clear from the well-known epigram: 'If I don't love you, Horace, more than my own life, may your friend look no better than a skinny mule!' But he spoke out much more strongly to Augustus in his last will and testament: 'Remember Horatius Flaccus as you will myself.'

Augustus even offered Horace the post of secretary, as can be seen from this letter of his to Maecenas: 'So far I have been able to write my letters to my friends myself, but now that I am too busy and in poor health I should like to take our friend Horace away from you. He will accordingly exchange the patronage of your table for that of my own, and will help me write my letters.' Even when Horace declined the offer Augustus was not offended and continued to cultivate his friendship. There are letters extant from which I have taken a few quotations to illustrate this. 'Make yourself at home in my house as if you shared it with me; it is quite right and proper for you to do so, for that was how I wanted things to be between us had your health permitted.' And again: 'You can also hear from our friend Septimius how much I have you in mind, for I happened to mention you in his hearing. Even if your pride made you despise my friendship, I shan't copy your haughty ways in return.' Furthermore, amongst other teasing epithets he often called Horace a 'chaste little dick' and a 'charming little fellow', and he enriched him by more than one act of generosity. As for his writings, Augustus thought so highly of them and was so sure that they would live for all time that he commissioned him not only to write the Centennial Hymn but also to celebrate the victory of his stepsons Tiberius and Drusus over the Vindelici, thereby obliging him to add a fourth book of lyrics to his other three after a long interval. And after reading some of the *sermones* the emperor protested at finding no mention of himself: 'You must know that I am cross with you for not addressing me rather than anyone else in your many writings of this kind. Can you be afraid that your reputation will suffer in later times because you appear to be my friend?' This produced the poem addressed to Augustus which starts:

Since you carry so many weighty affairs on your shoulders,
strengthening Rome's defences, promoting decent behaviour,
reforming our laws, it would damage the public interest, Caesar,
if I were to waste your time with a lengthy conversation.[1]

1. *Epistles* II.1.1.ff.

Physically Horace was short and plump, just as he is described by himself in his satires[2] and by Augustus in this letter: 'Onysius has brought me your little book, which I accept in good part, small as it is, as making your excuses. But you seem to me to fear that your books will be bigger than you are yourself, though it is height you lack, not bulk. You are therefore permitted to write on a pint pot, so that your volume may be pot-bellied like yourself.'

He is believed to have been rather free in sexual practices, for it is said that he had his women placed in a room lined with mirrors in such a way that wherever he looked he could see a reflection of his love-making. He lived mostly in his country retreat, on his Sabine farm or in Tibur, where a house near the small grove of Tiburnus is pointed out as his . . .[3] I have in my possession some elegiacs attributed to him and a prose letter, purporting to be a recommendation of himself to Maecenas, but neither, I think, are genuine; the elegiacs are commonplace and the letter obscurely phrased, and obscurity was certainly no fault of his.

Horace was born on the sixth day before the Ides of December in the consulship of Lucius Cotta and Lucius Torquatus,[4] and died on the fifth day before the Kalends of December during the consulship of Gaius Marcius Censorinus and Gaius Asinius Gallus,[5] fifty-nine days after the death of Maecenas. He was in his fifty-seventh year. He named Augustus as his heir before witnesses when he was too ill to be able to make and sign a will. He was laid to rest in a grave at the far end of the Esquiline Hill, close to the tomb of Maecenas.

2. *Epistles* I.4.15, I.20.24. 'Satires' is used loosely to cover all Horace's hexameters.
3. A gap.in the MSS seems likely, as there is no mention of Horace's genuine works.
4. 8 December 65 B.C.
5. 27 November 8 B.C.

# NOTES

# EPODES

## I

This poem was written just before the battle of Attium when it was expected that Maecenas would join Octavian (later Augustus): in the event he stayed in Rome.

1–2. The Roman fleet consisted mainly of small *Liburnian galleys*: these would be superior in speed and manoeuvrability to ships large and heavy enough to have *towering bulwarks*.

29. Sheep were pastured in the plains of *Calabria* during winter, and driven up to the hills of *Lucania* in summer.

31. *Circean*: because Tusculum was founded by Telegonus, son of Ulysses and Circe.

## 2

8. The Senate and the law-courts were housed in the *Forum*.

9–10. Grapevines were trained to grow on trees. This vegetable union is compared to a marriage.

53. i.e. 'when there are easterly gales'.

55. *African fowl*: guinea-fowl.

71. The *Ides* were the thirteenth or fifteenth and the *Kalends* the first day of the month.

## 3

8. *Canidia*: a witch (see also epodes 5 and 17).

9. *Argonauts' captain*: Jason.

## 4

12. *the crier*: an officer who during the flogging proclaimed the offence to the onlookers.

15–16. L. Roscius *Otho* carried a law in 67 B.C. that the first

fourteen rows in the Theatre (next to the 'orchestra' where sena-
tors sat) should be reserved for knights (*equites*), and so on accord-
ing to degree.

18. *beaked*: see note on III.1.39.

19. This refers to the way Sextus Pompeius manned his fleet (cf.
epode 9, line 10).

# 5

5. *Lucina*: the name applied to Juno in her role of goddess of
childbirth.

7,13. The *purple*-edged toga was worn by boys until they
assumed the all-white toga at about fifteen. The parti-coloured
toga and a gold amulet were the *emblems* of boyhood.

55. *Diana*: the 'dark' side of the goddess is meant here – Hecate,
as she was called in the underworld.

61. *Subura*: a street of bad repute in Rome.

*the ancient rake:* presumably this designation, and all mascu-
line or second-person pronouns down to line 87, refer to Canidia's
'lover' Varus – see line 77.

73. *perfumed*: presumably with preparations that make him
*oblivious*.

# 6

5. *Molossian . . . Laconian* (Spartan): highly regarded strains.

# 7

2. Note the 'cinematic' close-up.

8. *the Sacred Way (Via Sacra)*: the triumphal route in Rome.

# 8

15–18. *Stoic pamphlets* would recommend a rational approach to
life and indifference to reverses of fortune.

18. *hamptons*: Cockney rhyming slang – not Hampton Court,
but Hampton Wick.

# 9

3. *Caesar's triumph*: Octavian's at Actium.

6–11. *As when . . . his friends*: Sextus Pompeius, defeated by Agrippa near Messana in 36 B.C., fled to Lesbos and Asia, where he was captured and executed by Antony. He called himself 'son of *Neptune*'.

10. *slaves*: cf. epode 4, line 19.

12. *stakes*: these were to construct a palisade when pitching camp.

15. *eunuchs*: the term is directed at Cleopatra's lieutenants.

17. The *Gauls* are the Celtic Galatians of Asia Minor who deserted to Octavian before the battle.

20,22. *Hail Triumph (io Triumphe)*: the spectators' usual shout at a triumph.

23. Marius led the Numidian king *Jugurtha* in a triumph in 104 B.C.

33. *seasick*: Horace and Maecenas did not participate in or observe the battle of Actium – there is no reason to suppose they were even afloat at the time. The Latin word *nausea*, which Horace employs, can denote seasickness specifically or nausea generally. Perhaps his own description of events at sea has caused Horace to affect to feel vicariously queasy. But the queasiness could as well be real, caused by copious drinking – cf. the demand for *larger goblets* in line 31. In any case, strong wine (such as *Caecuban*) was a known remedy for nausea – cf. Pliny, *Natural History*, 23.43.

# 10

14. This refers not to the famous Ajax, brother of Teucer, but to *Ajax* son of Oileus, king of Locris. He had dragged Cassandra (a prophetess and daughter of Priam) from *Pallas* Athene's altar – hence the goddess' revenge.

# 11

13. *injudicious God's*: Bacchus'.

22. It was a conventional posture of the unrequited lover to lie stretched out at the beloved's threshold.

# 13

6. *Torquatus*: see Glossary: Manlius.

9. The lyres are called *Cyllenean* because they are sacred to Mercury, their inventor, who was born on Mt Cyllene in Arcadia.

11. The *stalwart foster-child* was Achilles, whose education was entrusted to Chiron, a *Centaur* famous for his knowledge of archery, music and medicine.

# 14

8. The *lines long promised* are presumably the *Epodes* – they are described as iambic, the *Epodes'* predominant metre.

14. *that*: i.e. Helen's *flame*.

# 16

7. The Germanic Cimbri and Teutones were eventually defeated by Marius in 102–101 B.C.

43. A reference to the persistent fantasy that somewhere amid the ocean the 'blessèd islands', an earthly pardise, existed.

58. *extremes*: of rain and drought.

59–60. The *Argo* was the ship of the Argonauts, commanded by Jason. The *queen of Colchis* was Medea, who assisted Jason and left Colchis with him.

# 17

2. *Proserpina's realm*: the underworld, of which Proserpina was queen.

3. He calls upon the 'dark' *Diana* of witchcraft, i.e. Hecate.

7. This was a magic *wheel* whose spinning would draw a lover to the house. If the spinning was *reversed*, the spell was broken.

8–10. *Nereus* was the father of Thetis, and hence the grandfather of Achilles, who wounded with a spear *Telephus*, king of the *Mysians*, and then healed him (as had been foretold by an oracle) with rust from the same weapon.

11–14. Priam, *the king* of Troy, *left* his city and knelt to *Achilles* to beg for the return of the body of his son *Hector*, whom the Greek had killed.

15–18. The enchantress *Circe* turned into swine the companions (*oarsmen*) of *Ulysses*. The hero became her lover, and persuaded her to give them back their humanity.

28,29,60. *Sabellian . . . Marsian . . . Paelignian*: witches seem to have abounded among these indigenous Italian mountain tribes.

42–3. *Castor* and his *brother* (Pollux) blinded the poet Stesichorus for slandering their sister *Helen*. Subsequently Stesichorus retracted by writing in a palinode that Helen never went to Troy, and thus regained his sight.

47. *nine-day ashes*: all funeral rites were completed on or by the ninth day after death.

49–51. *Pactumeius* was the genuine name of a Roman *gens* (clan). Perhaps the surprising statement made in line 51 is meant to throw doubt on those made in 49 and 50.

55. *Cotyttian*: pertaining to Cotytto, a Thracian goddess whose mysteries seem to have involved a degree of licentiousness – cf. *liberating* (from constraint) *Bacchus* in line 56.

65. *Pelops* was *treacherous* for having won a chariot race by bribing his rival's charioteer, but then refusing to pay up.


# ODES, BOOK I

## I

4. The *post* was a marker round which the racing chariots turned or *swerved*

8. *triple honours*: curule aedileship, praetorship and consulship – the maximum official honours to which a Roman could aspire.

9. *everything*: corn, chaff, dust, everything.

## 2

1. *The Father*: the father of the gods, i.e. Jupiter, Jove.

14. *the Tuscan shore*: the right-hand shore, since Tuscany was located to the north of Rome.

15–19. *Numa*: Numa Pompilius (second king of Rome, Romulus' immediate successor) built a palace and a temple to *Vesta* on the *left bank* of the Tiber. *Ilia* became the wife of the river-god Tiber by being thrown into his waters – hence *uxorious*.

33–6. *Venus* was the mother of Aeneas, the legendary founder of the Roman state. *Mars* was *our sponsor* as the father of Romulus.

41–4. Here Horace suggests that Octavian (later Augustus) may be an earthly manifestation of the god *Mercury*: Octavian was the heir and adopted son of *Julius Caesar* – and was indeed, as a young man, at the battle of Philippi, his *avenger*. The audacious compliment is re-affirmed in the last line of the poem.

52. *Caesar* here refers to Octavian (as opposed to line 44).

## 3

2. *Helen's brothers*: Castor and Pollux.

## 4

2. Ships were beached during the winter months.

17–18. At drinking parties it was customary to choose, by casting dice, one of the party to act as a sort of master of ceremonies. His duties were to choose the wines, determine the order of their drinking, and so forth.

## 5

14–16. The *plaque* is a mark of Horace's gratitude to Neptune that he has been saved from drowning in the sea (of Pyrrha's anger).

# 6

6. *Peleus' son* was Achilles.

9. *Pelops' cruel house* included Agamemnon, Orestes and Electra. The working out of their destinies was a favourite theme of the Greek tragedians (cf. Aeschylus' *Oresteia*).

# 7

1–4. A catalogue of illustrious names such as furnished the subject-matter of conservative, mythologically inclined poets contemporary with Horace.

6–7. The *olive* was traditionally associated with *Pallas* Athene.

21–32. On his return to his native *Salamis* after the Trojan war, *Teucer* was banished by *his father* because he had 'allowed' his brother, Ajax, to die. There is perhaps some irony in Horace's dwelling upon the fate of Teucer since L. Munatius *Plancus* (consul in 42 B.C.), the addressee of this poem, was alleged to have proscribed his own brother: thus he shared with Teucer the taint of fratricide. Cf. Introduction, p.30.

29. This second *Salamis* was founded by Teucer in Cyprus.

# 8

3. *Sybaris* was a Greek colony in southern Italy which became a byword for luxurious living. Thus, by dubbing him Sybaris, Horace says in effect that the young man has gone soft, become unmanly.

4. *the sun-baked plain*: the Field of Mars, where Roman men exercised and trained.

9–10. The Romans rubbed *olive oil* into their skins before undertaking athletic activity. They considered *vipers' blood* to be a deadly poison.

13–16. The sea-goddess *Thetis* was Achilles' mother. According to legend, she dressed her son as a young woman, hoping that he would thus avoid the muster for the war at Troy, where she knew he was doomed to die. (Thus Horace equates the infatuate youth with the disguised hero.) *Lycia*, in Asia Minor, sent troops to assist in the defence of Troy.

# 9

On different interpretations; see Introduction, p.20.

# 10

13–16. This stanza refers to Priam's visit to Achilles to recover the body of his son Hector (cf. *Iliad* 24).

# 11

3. *Babylonian calculations*: Chaldean astrological forecasts.

# 12

This poem shows something of the triadic structure apparent in the Centennial Hymn. See the introductory note, p.221.

14. *the Father*: of the gods, i.e. Jupiter.

22. *the Virgin*: Diana.

24. The archery of *Phoebus* (Apollo) in his inimical aspect brought blight and disease.

25. *Alcides*: Hercules.

   *Leda's boys*: Castor and Pollux.

34. *Pompilius*: Numa (cf. note on I.2.15–19).

35. *fasces*: bundles of rods (or rods and an axe) emblematical of magisterial authority. *Tarquin* refers to Tarquinius Superbus, the last of the kings of Rome, whose fall in 510 B.C. led to the foundation of the Republic. *Cato* the Younger: see Glossary.

40–44. *Fabricius, Curius* and *Camillus* were eminent men in the early history of Rome, chosen here as exemplars of the old republican virtues.

45. The family of the Marcelli was distinguished from the Punic wars onward. One *Marcellus* was an eminent general against Hannibal. Another was the son-in-law of Augustus.

47. *the Julian constellation*: the successors of Julius Caesar, of whom Octavian/Augustus was one.

49–50. *Father . . . son of Saturn*: Jupiter. The three *Fates* collaborated to spin destiny in the form of a thread.

60. *polluted*: by 'heathen' or sacrilegious rites.

## 13

1–12. Note the underlying culinary metaphor. The *liver* was the seat of love's passion. Cf. I.25.15.

## 14

1. *ship*: i.e. (most plausibly) of State.

14. *icons (pictis puppibus)*: presumably auspicious images painted on the stern.

17. Perhaps Horace refers here to the time when he served the republican party under Brutus.

## 15

1. *faithless shepherd*: Paris.

33–6. The *wrath* of the *Myrmidons* on behalf of Achilles (see Glossary: Briseis) is here taken to have delayed the sack of Troy.

## 16

5–6. *Pythian*: pertaining to Delphi, where Apollo spoke his oracles through the ecstatic Pythia, his priestess.

9. *Noric*: Noricum, between the Danube and the Alps, was a district famous for its steel.

## 17

12. *that sweet piping*: of Faunus, i.e. Pan.

18–19. The *Teian lyre* was that of the poet Anacreon, since he was born in the island of Teos.

19–20. *Penelope* and *Circe* were respectively the patient, faithful wife and distracting enchantress of Ulysses on his return through many adventures from the Trojan War (cf. Homer's *Odyssey*).

22. *Thyoneus* was an epithet of Bacchus, whose mother was *Semele*.

## 18

1. *Varus*: either Quinctilius Varus (probably the Quintilius of I.24) or P. Alfenus Varus (the Alfenus of Catullus' *Poems* 30).

14. *Fox's-Pelt*: Bacchus, who is here called 'Bassareus', a Greek epithet meaning 'wearer of the fox-skin'.

## 19

1. *mother*: Venus.

2. *son:* Bacchus.

12. *bold in flight*: a standard Parthian tactic was by feigning retreat to lure the enemy into an attack which was duly showered with arrows ('Parthian shots').

13. *put living turf*: the usual method of making an outdoor altar.

## 20

1. *You'll drink*: i.e. 'when you visit me at my Sabine farm'.

3–8. The reference is to Maecenas' first entry into the Theatre after recovering from an illness (cf. II.17.25–6).

## 21

7–8. *Algidus . . . Erymanthus . . . Cragus*: mountains in Latium, Arcadia and Lycia respectively.

12. Apollo's *brother* was Mercury, who invented the *lyre*.

## 24

6. Quinctilius Varus of Cremona died in 24 B.C.

## 27

8. At table it was customary to recline on *couches* rather than sit on chairs.

17. *freeborn*: not born a slave. Horace's father was a freedman.

21. *Thessalian drugs*: Thessaly was notorious for witchcraft.

# 28

It has been maintained that this ode is actually two discrete poems, consisting of (a) the first five and (b) the last four stanzas. I believe that this division is inadmissible because *none* of the MSS show such a break, and (b) commences *me quoque* ('me too') – thus (b) must follow on from something, and it would surely be perverse to speculate that that something is anything other than (a). Nevertheless, the poem does fall into two distinct 'movements', each of which has a beginning, a middle and an end: (a) is a meditation addressed to Archytas on the inevitability of death; (b) is a dramatic scena addressed to an anonymous sailor in which a dead soul pleads and threatens in order to gain admittance from limbo into the underworld; in (a) the allusions are integral to the development of the theme, whereas in (b) they are more incidental or even decorative. I conclude that the piece is one poem (the 'speaker' throughout being the drowned man of (b)), but a poem in the form of a diptych, as it were, the two 'panels' being hinged upon the phrase *me quoque*.

7. *Pelops' father*: Tantalus.

10–15. *Euphorbus*; a Trojan hero in the war against the Greeks. Pythagoras, a Greek philosopher who advanced the theory of 'metempsychosis', the transmigration of souls, believed himself to be a reincarnation of Euphorbus (among others). He proved his claim by recognizing an old shield in Argos as the one he had used at Troy – when the shield was examined, the name Euphorbus was found on its inside. Pythagoras flourished about 500 years before Horace.

23–24, 35–36. Until the dead body was formally buried, the soul was condemned to wander in limbo and not be received into the underworld. The scattering of *three handfuls of earth* constituted formal burial.

# 29

1–4. An unsuccessful expedition was made into Arabia Felix (Sabaea) in 24 B.C.

8. Like an oriental Cupid.

10. *cupbearer*: as though he were Iccius' Ganymede (and thus rather more than his cupbearer).

## 31

The dedication of Apollo's temple on the Palatine took place in 28 B.C.

17. *Son of Latona*: Apollo.

## 32

4. *barbitos*: the Lesbian lyre.

5. *Lesbos' citizen*: Alcaeus (see Glossary: Lesbos).

13. The Lesbian lyre was indeed made in part from a *tortoise-shell*.

## 34

2–3. *an ignorant wisdom*: Epicureanism.

4. *gone about*: 'going about' is the manoeuvre by which one changes from one tack to the next when sailing into the wind.

15. *shrill susurration*: the creaking and whirring of Fortune's wings.

## 35

1. *Fortuna* had two statues at Antium, a town on the coast a little south of Rome.

17. The Oxford text reads *serva necessitas* ('servant Necessity'). Some MSS have *saeva* ('cruel') instead of *serva* – an alternative which has the merit of suggesting the image of the lictors preceding the magistrate, carrying instruments of torture and correction.

21. The priests of Fides (Faith, *Loyalty*) performed sacrifices with the right hand *swathed* in a band of *white* cloth.

30. Augustus proposed to visit Britain in 27 B.C. – but the plan proved abortive.

33. *fratricides*: a reference to the recent civil wars.

## 36

8. This line is potentially contentious: it translates *rex* ('king') as 'tutor', though this seems to be the only example of the word being

used in this sense. However, 'tutor' is the likeliest (i.e. most plausible) meaning yet proposed.

9. Roman boys wore a purple-fringed toga. At about fifteen they changed this for the all-white 'toga of manhood' (*toga virilis*).

# 37

This poem refers to the defeat of Cleopatra (and Mark Antony) by Octavian (later Augustus) at the battle of Actium in 31 B.C.

3. *Salian delicacies*: a feast served on special occasions to the images of Mars. (Salii: 'jumpers', the dancing priests of Mars.)

12–13. In fact Antony's fleet burned; Cleopatra's fled.

16. *Mareotic* denotes here an Egyptian wine.

# ODES, BOOK II

## I

15. *Dalmatic Triumph*: Pollio was accorded a triumph in 39 B.C. for his defeat of the Parthini, an Illyrian people living on the borders of Dalmatia.

21–4. These lines refer perhaps to the battle of Pharsalus, where Julius Caesar defeated Pompey.

25. *Juno* was the tutelary goddess of Carthage.

26–8. At the battle of Thapsus (46 B.C.) in North Africa the Pompeian party and Cato were finally defeated. A century earlier, Roman armies under P. Scipio Africanus Minor had sacked Carthage. Many other Roman victories followed in the area, culminating with the death in 104 B.C. of the Numidian king Jugurtha.

38. *Cean*: Simonides (c. 556–c. 467 B.C.), the lyric poet of Ceos, was especially celebrated for his dirges and epitaphs.

40. *mode*: see note on III.9.11.

## 2

10–11. The Carthaginians (or *Punic* people) had settlements on both sides of the Straits of Gibraltar.

## 3

16. See Glossary: Fates.

26–8. The Romans drew lots from dockets *shaken* in an *urn*. The *little boat* is the craft in which the ferryman Charon transported the shades of the dead across the river Styx into the underworld.

## 4

6–8. The *captive girl* for whom *Agamemnon burned* at the fall of Troy was Cassandra, Priam's daughter, a prophetess.

10. *Thessaly's victor* was Achilles, whose father was Peleus, king of Thessaly (and an Argonaut), and who killed Hector, the eldest son of Priam.

## 5

2. *double yoke*: i.e. of marriage.

## 6

10–11. *skin-clad*: the sheep of Tarentum were so valuable that they were clothed in jackets to keep their fleeces clean and soft.

## 7

5–9. After Philippi many of Brutus' supporters (including Horace) were pardoned by Octavian (later Augustus). The restoration of full civil rights to this (unknown) *Pompeius* was presumably delayed because he continued for a time to support the beaten faction.

10. Horace fought on the 'wrong' side at Philippi, i.e. that of Brutus.

12–13. *words were eaten*: a more literal translation would be 'dust was bitten'.

14. This line refers satirically to Homer's habit of using divinities to rescue his heroes from military embarrassments.

23. Perfume was customarily kept in phials made from sea-shells.

25–6. For *master of wine* see note on I.4.17–18.

# 9

13. This line refers to Nestor, whose son, killed in the Trojan War, was Antilochus (cf. line 15).

# 10

19. Apollo's *archery*, when he turned it against man, brought disease and blight.

# 13

19. *dungeons*: Horace's expression is *Italum robur* ('Italian oak' or 'Italian strength'), which may mean something equivalent to the English 'heart of oak'. However, *robur* was used regularly to denote the dungeon of Rome (the Tullianum).

24. *Aeolian*: though a Lesbian, Sappho – and Alcaeus – used the Aeolic dialect. (See Glossary: Lesbos.)

28, 32. Alcaeus himself was exiled from Lesbos for his opposition to the tyrant Myrsilus, who was later driven out.

34. Cerberus – more usually credited with three heads.

# 14

9. Styx.

23. The *cypress* was associated, as in later times, with death and grieving.

## 15

4–5. Grapevines were usually trained upon (or 'married to') *elms*; *plane trees* were unsuitable for this purpose.

17. The *common turf* was protected because it was used to build outdoor altars and to roof cottages.

## 16

9–10. The *consul* was the military commander of Rome – his was the most senior magisterial office. The *lictor* walked before him on ceremonial occasions carrying the fasces – see note on I.12.35.

38. The *little farm* was the small Sabine estate presented to Horace by Maecenas.

39. *Grecian Muse*: see Glossary: Lesbos.

## 17

17–20. These lines refer to Maecenas' well-known interest in astrology – which Horace did not share.

25–6. See note on I.20. 3–8.

27. Cf. II.13.

## 18

13. *my powerful friend*: Maecenas, who had given Horace the *Sabine farm* referred to in line 12.

## I 19

13. Marooned by Theseus on Naxos, Ariadne was rescued and married by Bacchus, who gave her a crown of seven stars which became a constellation after her death.

29–32. Bacchus had gone into the underworld to bring back his mother Semele.

## 20

17. *dissimulating fear*: see note on I.19.12.

# ODES, BOOK III

## I

10. The *Campus* was the Campus Martius, or Field of Mars, where the Romans exercised and trained.

16. The Romans drew lots by shaking dockets in an *urn*.

20–21. An allusion to Damocles.

26. *Arcturus* and *Haedus* (the Kid) are constellations that set and rise in late and early October respectively.

31–2. The Dog-star (Canicula) was considered to *parch the field* in summer.

39. War-galleys were *bronze-beaked* by virtue of a metal-sheathed ram on the bow, at or below the water-line, the purpose of which was to hole and thus sink enemy vessels.

## 2

13. This is the celebrated line: '*Dulce et decorum est pro patria mori*' – 'the old lie', as Wilfred Owen called it.

29. *Ancient of Days*: Diespiter, Jupiter.

## 3

15–16. Having founded and become the first king of Rome, Romulus (*Quirinus*) was said to have disappeared in a thunder-storm in a chariot drawn by the horses of *Mars*, his father.

20,24. Paris was the *partial judge* who in his famous 'judgement' preferred Aphrodite (Venus) to Hera (Juno) and Athene (*Minerva*). His prize was Helen, the wife of Menelaus, king of Sparta.

21. Helen (see preceding note) was the *foreign woman* – Paris brought her to Troy.

25–6. The *egregious guest* and *Spartan adult'ress* were Paris (in Sparta) and Helen – see note on lines 20, 24 above.

31–6. Juno was the mother of Mars, who was the father, by Rhea Silvia – or Ilia, a *Trojan priestess* (see Glossary: Ilia) – of Romulus, *my hateful grandson*, the founder of Rome.

60. Augustus was rumoured to have contemplated at one time moving the seat of government from Rome to the east.

# 4

9–16. These names from the region around Venusia would have been quite unfamiliar to a metropolitan Roman.

41–2. These lines are the fulcrum of the poem. Having refreshed Caesar by the performance of some work(s) of art (cf. line 37), the Muses now give him *lene consilium*, 'calm wisdom' or advice. They turn from aesthetics to the policies of Rome, the two domains being united by resting upon order, proportion, harmony – principles the Muses well understand. The artefact (as it were) to be achieved by Augustus is an ordered peace, and his pursuit of this end is as glorious as Jove's suppression of the disorderly revolt of the Giants/Titans: thus the last 38 lines of the poem constitute one sustained metaphor.

45. *him who controls*: Jupiter.

49. *progeny*: see Glossary: Giants and Titans.

63–4. The places named are associated with Apollo. He had an oracle at *Patara* on the river Xanthus in *Lycia* (south of Troy). The island of *Delos* was his birthplace.

73–6. See Glossary: Giants.

# 5

10. *the sacred shields*: these were kept by the Salii (priests of Mars) and symbolized the stability of the empire.

11. *toga*: the proper and proudly worn dress of a Roman citizen.

# 6

14. At the battle of Actium archers from *Dacia* fought alongside Cleopatra's Egyptians.

23. *to her dainty fingernails*: a more conventional rendering would be 'from her tenderest years' (i.e. from the time when her finger-

nails were tender). For an interesting argument which supports my reading cf. p. 66 of Gordon Williams' *Third Book of Horace's Odes* (Oxford, 1969).

# 7

6. The constellation of *the Goat* rises at the end of September, a season of storms.

26–8. Exercise on the *Field of Mars* was usually followed by bathing *in the Tiber*.

# 8

1–4. The *Kalends of March* was the Matronalia, a festival celebrated by married women in honour of Juno in her role of goddess of childbirth. Lines 3–4 refer to sacrifice on an outdoor altar.

6. Cf. II.13.

11. It was thought that smoking the jar helped the wine to mature.

21. The Cantabri were defeated in 29 B.C.

# 9

11. Greek and Roman music employed a number of *modes*, each of which was clearly associated with specific emotions. One mode differed from another approximately as major differs from minor in tonal music. (The word *modos* is translated here as 'modes' on the assumption that its denotation of measure or quantity can apply to discriminations of pitch.)

# 10

3–20. It was a conventional posture of the unrequited lover to lie stretched out at the beloved's threshold.

10. Horace does not specify any particular implement or machine, yet the image is vivid and its relevance plain.

## 11

3–4. The barbitos, the lyre of Lesbos, made from *tortoise-shell*.

15–16. *Cerberus* so *succumbed* when Orpheus entered the underworld to attempt to rescue from death his wife Eurydice.

33. *Just one*: Hypermnestra.

## 12

The soliloquy form (Neobule addresses herself) is unique in Horace, as is the metre of this poem.

## 13

3. Horace will celebrate the Fontinalia (13 October).

9. The *Dog-Days*, i.e. the days of the Dog-star (Canicula), were usually reputed to be the hottest.

## 14

1–4. Augustus returned from his Spanish campaign, in the course of which he contracted a serious illness, in 25 B.C.

18. The *Marsian troubles* were the Social War (91 or 90–88 B.C.) between Rome and the Italian allies (*Socii*) over the question of franchise. It was inconclusive, but full Roman citizenship was later granted to all the Italians.

28. *Plancus was consul* in 42 B.C., the year of the battle of Philippi, when Horace was twenty-three.

## 15

13–16. The point is that at her age Chloris should occupy herself with domesticity, not dissipation.

# 16

11–12. The *Argive prophet* was Amphiarius. He was persuaded by his wife to take part in the expedition of the Seven against Thebes, which he knew would end in disaster. She in turn had been bribed by Polynices, rightful king of Thebes.

13. The *Macedonian* was Philip II (father of Alexander the Great), who gained possession of many Greek cities by bribery.

20. Maecenas preferred to remain an influential *eques* (knight) instead of moving into the professional, senatorial class.

34–5. *Laestrygonian jars* contained the wine of Formiae, founded by Lamus, legendary king of the Laestrygonians.

# 18

10. *Nones of December*: the Faunalia were celebrated on 5 December.

# 19

14–17. There were *nine . . . Muses* and *three* Graces.

# 20

15. *the boy shanghai'd*: Ganymede.

# 22

1. *Virgin*: Diana.

2–3. Diana shared with Juno the function of presiding over childbirth.

4. In heaven, Luna (the moon); on earth, Diana; in the underworld, Hecate.

# 23

20. *sputtering*: because thrown on the fire.

## 24

1. *intact*: because untouched by Rome.

3. Many editors read *terrenum* ('mainland') for *Tyrrhenum* ('Tuscan').

4. I follow the alternative reading *publicum* ('common') for *Apulicum*, since no one built grand villas on the coast of Apulia.

28. *Father of Cities*: a reference to Augustus, who was called *pater patriae* ('father of his country').

57. Things *Greek* were liable to be thought vicious or effeminate. A *hoop* was a favourite gift from a young man to the boy he loved.

## 26

3–8. The *arms* etc. are dedicated to Venus and hung up in her temple like trophies.

7. The *levers and axes* were to break down the door where gentler means (e.g. the *lyre* of line 5) had failed to gain admittance. (I prefer Bentley's *secures* to the *arcus* of the MSS since axes would provide a more practicable means of forcing entry than would bows and arrows.)

9–10. According to one version of the legend, Venus was first washed ashore at Paphos, in *Cyprus*. One of her many temples was at *Memphis*, in Egypt.

## 27

15. The *left* was the unlucky side in augury.

25. *So* denotes (presumably) in similar weather, at the same season, with equivalent imprudence. Since Horace rehearses the story at considerable length (52 lines), one surmises that there may have been some further analogy or parallel between Europa's case and that of 'Galatea': if so, it is lost.

40–2. According to Homer, truly prophetic dreams come to the sleeper through the gate of horn, mere fantasies through that of *ivory*.

## 28

2. The Neptunalia were celebrated on 23 July.

13–16. *praise her*: Venus. The island of *Cnidos* was associated with her, and according to one legend she was first washed ashore at *Paphos*, in Cyprus.

## 29

5. *my estate*: his Sabine farm, Maecenas' gift.

17–19. *Andromeda's . . . father* was Cepheus, king of Ethiopia, who gave his name to a star. Cepheus, *Procyon* and *Leo* all rise in July.

34. *a river*: e.g. the Tiber.

62. *his twin*: Castor.

## 30

13. See Glossary: Lesbos.

# CENTENNIAL HYMN

In 17 B.C. Augustus re-instituted the Secular Games, a festival celebrating the preservation of the State which was intended to be held every eleventh decade (*saeculum*): see lines 21–4. On the third and final day of the Games, an ode was sung in Apollo's temple by a choir of boys and girls. Horace was commissioned to write it: the result was this Centennial Hymn.

The stanzas of the Hymn are grouped into six triads (plus one stanza by way of a coda), each triad being unified thematically. This arrangement points the poem's connection with the choric forms of the Greeks (e.g. Pindar), whose odes proceeded in triads of strophe, antistrophe and epode.

8. *the Seven Hills*: of Rome.

9. *Sun*: Apollo (Phoebus).

13–16. *Ilithyia* was a Greek goddess of childbirth. *Lucina* was

Juno's name in this same capacity. *Genitalis* ('bringer of birth') is a title not found elsewhere.

17. *Goddess*: Diana, in her role of goddess of childbirth.

18–20. In the hope of increasing the population, Augustus introduced legislation that laid a heavy tax on bachelors – to little avail.

35. *Luna*: Diana in her role of goddess of the moon.

49. *he of Anchises' and Venus' pure blood*: Augustus. Horace credits him with direct descent from Anchises and Venus since they were the parents of Aeneas.

71. *Fifteen Men*: the keepers of the prophetic Sybilline Books, who had charge of the Secular Games.

# ODES, BOOK IV

## I

2. *so long*: ten years (23–13 B.C.) had elapsed since the publication of *Odes* I, II and III, *Epistles* I and II intervening.

12. See note on I.13.1–12.

40. See note on III.7.26–8.

## 2

1. *Julus* Antonius, son of Mark Antony by Fulvia (brought up by his stepmother Octavia), obtained Augustus' favour and was consul in 10 B.C. He is reported to have written an epic poem: Horace tactfully suggests that he is better qualified to compose a victory ode on Augustus' expected return from Gaul in late 16 B.C.

2–4. See Glossary: Icarus.

11. *dithyrambs*: Greek choral odes, originally sung in honour of Dionysus (Bacchus). Pindar's are composed in exceptionally free verse and audacious style.

13–16. The reference is to paeans, hymns in honour of gods and heroes, such as Theseus who fought with the Lapiths against the *Centaurs*, and Bellerophon who killed the *Chimaera*.

18. *the Elean palm*: the palm awarded to victors at Olympic

games, which are celebrated in some of Pindar's odes. (*Elean* because Olympia was in Elis.)

25. *swan of Dirce*: Pindar. *Dirce* was a spring near Thebes, and therefore near the birthplace of Pindar.

32. Horace refers to the intricacy of the numerous metres he adopted or adapted from Alcaeus and Sappho (see Glossary: Lesbos) and employed in the *Odes*.

43-4. The law-courts were in the *Forum* and were closed on occasions of public rejoicing.

50. See note on epode 9, lines 20–22.

## 3

3. The *Isthmian* games took place on alternate years on the Isthmus of Corinth.

8. *Delian* wreaths were of laurel (or 'bays') which was sacred to Apollo, whose birthplace was the island of Delos.

12. *Aeolian*: because Horace's models Alcaeus and Sappho (see Glossary: Lesbos) wrote in the Aeolic dialect.

17. *Pierian virgin*: the Muse (Euterpe or Melpomene).

22. *pointed out*: as the commissioned author of the Centennial Hymn, cf. introductory note p.221.

## 4

A neo-Pindaric ode to celebrate the victories of Augustus' stepsons in 15 B.C.

2. *king of the Gods*: Jupiter.

28. *Neros*: Tiberius (later emperor) and Drusus, Augustus' stepsons.

37-44. C. Claudius Nero (ancestor of the *Neros* of line 28) defeated *Hasdrubal* at the *river Metaurus* in 207 B.C., the first Roman victory over the Carthaginians after a series of defeats. The *dire Carthaginian* was Hannibal.

73. The *Claudian* family was interrelated with the Julian, of which Augustus was a member.

## 5

Written during Augustus' absence in Gaul and Spain from 16 to 13 B.C.

21–4. Augustus enacted severe laws against adultery.

29–32. This stanza presents rather an idealized picture of idyllic independence for Horace's time: landowners whose farms were their homes were rare under Augustan 'capitalism'.

30. The Romans trained their grapevines to grow on trees: prior to such a 'marriage' the trees were *lonely* bachelors.

31–6. The worship of Augustus as a demi-god was encouraged. The Senate decreed that libations should be poured to him at private meals as well as public banquets.

## 6

1. *God*: Phoebus (Apollo) – see line 26.

11–12. Achilles was killed by Paris aided by Apollo.

13. The Greeks sailed away from Troy leaving behind a great wooden *horse*, which the Trojans dragged into their city as the Greeks had expected. At night the men hidden inside the horse emerged and opened the gates to their returning fellows. Troy was sacked.

22. *your*: Phoebus'.

23–4. *other walls*: those of Rome.

31. Horace now addresses the choir (of girls and boys) which is to perform his Centennial Hymn – see note on line 42 below.

33. *Delian Goddess*: Diana. She (and her brother Apollo) were born on the island of Delos.

35. *Lesbian*: see Glossary: Lesbos.

36. Horace probably speaks figuratively, and should not be thought of as literally playing the lyre and coaching the choir.

37. *Latona's son*: Apollo (Phoebus).

42. *the hymn*: Horace's Centennial Hymn – see the introductory note thereto on p.221.

# 7

3–4. Winter's floods have subsided.

25–8. *Hippolytus*, the son of *Theseus*, king of Athens, was fanatically *celibate*, and worshipped only Artemis (*Diana*): his stepmother Phaedra, who desired him, contrived his violent death. *Theseus* and his friend *Pirithous*, king of the Lapiths, attempted to abduct Proserpina from the underworld, of which she was queen: *Pirithous* was caught and bound in chains.

# 8

17–19. P. Scipio Africanus Maior defeated the Carthaginians, finally crushing Hannibal at the battle of Zama in 202 B.C. His adopted grandson and namesake Scipio Africanus Minor destroyed Carthage in 146 B.C.

20. *Calabrian Muses*: Q. Ennius, 'the father of Roman poetry', was born in Calabria and wrote on the wars with Carthage in his epic *Annals*.

22–3. *the son of Ilia and Mars*: Romulus.

31. *Tyndarides*: (sons of Tyndarus) Castor and Pollux.

# 9

10–11. *Aeolian girl*: Sappho, who wrote in the Aeolic dialect.

# 12

11–12. The *God* concerned is Pan, whose traditional home was *Arcadia*, a wild and mountainous region in the middle of the Greek Peloponnese.

13. This *Virgilius* is not the poet Virgil, who had died before the publication of this fourth book of Odes, and with regard to whom line 14 would be meaningless.

18. *Sulpician warehouse*: public vaults or warehouses which were presumably named after the builder or owner.

## 13

13. The island of Cos was noted for its fine silks.

## 14

14. *older Nero*: Tiberius, later emperor, the older stepson of Augustus, victorious over the tribes of the upper Rhine in 15 B.C.

29. *Claudius*: Tiberius – see note above.

34. *the very day*: i.e. precisely fifteen years after the final victory of Octavian (later Augustus) over Antony and Cleopatra in 30 B.C.

## 15

6–7. See III.5.5–12 and Glossary: Crassus.

9. *Arcade of Janus*: this arcade in Rome had two entrances which were kept open during wars and closed in peacetime: it was said to have been closed three times in Augustus' reign, and only twice before.

10. Perhaps a reference to Augustus' severe laws against adultery.

22. *Julian edicts*: laws promulgated by the Julian house, of which Augustus was a member.

31–2. *Anchises* and *Venus* were the parents of Aeneas: thus their *progeny* were the Roman people.

# GLOSSARY
# OF
# PROPER
# NAMES

ACHAEA   A Roman province in the northern part of the Peloponnese.

ACHAEMENES   Founder of Persia's first royal house, ancestor of Cyrus.

ACHERON   One of the four rivers of the underworld.

ACHERONTIA   A small town in Apulia.

ACHILLES   A Greek hero who took part (and died) in the Trojan war. He killed Hector, Priam's eldest son. His father was Peleus, an Argonaut and king of Thessaly; his mother Thetis, a sea-goddess; his tutor Chiron, a centaur.

ACRISIUS   See Danaë.

ACTIUM   The sea and land battle at which the combined forces of Mark Antony and Cleopatra were decisively beaten by those of Octavian (later Augustus) in 31 B.C.

AEACUS   King of Aegina, a son of Zeus (Jupiter). His descendants included Achilles and Ajax. A just ruler, he was made one of the three judges of the dead in the underworld.

AEFULA   A town in Latium (the district about Rome).

AELIUS   See Lamia.

AENEAS   A Trojan hero, son of Anchises and Venus. When Troy was sacked he and his family escaped, with some other Trojans, and sailed to Italy. There (according to one legend) under

Aeneas' direction, they founded the city of Rome. (Hence Aeneas is 'our father' in IV.7.15.) These events form the subject of Virgil's epic, the *Aeneid*.

**AEOLIAN**    Sappho and Alcaeus use the Aeolic dialect.

**AFRICANUS**    (a) P. Scipio Africanus Maior defeated the Carthaginians, finally crushing Hannibal at the battle of Zama in 202 B.C.

(b) His adopted grandson and namesake (Scipio Africanus Minor) destroyed Carthage in 146 B.C.

**AGAMEMNON**    Son of Atreus; brother of Menelaus; commander of the Greek forces at Troy.

**AGRIPPA**    M. Vipsanius Agrippa, Augustus' war minister.

**AGYIEUS**    A Greek epithet of Apollo (Phoebus), meaning 'guardian of the streets'.

**AJAX**    (a) A Greek hero participating (and dying) in the siege of Troy; son of Telamon, king of Salamis; brother of Teucer.

(b) Son of Oileus, king of Locris; he dragged Cassandra (a prophetess and daughter of Priam) from Pallas Athene's altar.

**ALBAN**    The Alban lake (Lago di Albano) lies about fifty miles south-east of Rome in the Alban hills. The region produced a highly regarded wine.

**ALBUNEA**    A prophetess to whom a spring and grotto near Tibur were sacred.

**ALCAEUS**    Greek lyric poet of Lesbos (q.v.); fl. 610 BC

**ALGIDUS**    A mountain in Latium.

**ALLOBROX**    The Allobroges were a Gallic tribe in the Rhône region. In 63 B.C. Catiline tried to incite them to rebel against Rome: they rejected his overtures – but two years later rebelled just the same.

**ALYATTES**    King of Lydia; son of Croesus.

**AMPHION**    Legendary builder of Thebes. The sound of his lyre made the stones come together of their own accord.

**ANACREON**    Greek lyric poet born in Teos; fl. in the mid-sixth century B.C.; famous for his verses on the themes of wine, woman and song.

**ANCHISES**    Anchises and Venus were the parents of Aeneas, who founded the state of Rome.

**ANCUS**    Marcius Ancus, the fourth king of Rome.

**ANTIOCHUS**    Antiochus III, 'the Great', conquered most of Asia

Minor, but was defeated by P. Scipio Asiaticus in 190 or 189 B.C.

ANTIUM   A town on the coast a little south of Rome.

ANTONIUS   Julus Antonius, son of Mark Antony and Fulvia, brought up by his stepmother Octavia; consul in 10 B.C.

APOLLO (PHOEBUS)   God of the sun; archer; patron of poetry and the Muses. His famous oracle was located at Delphi.

APULIA   A wild district, where Horace was born, in the southeast of Italy.

AQUILO   North wind.

ARCADIA   A wild and mountainous region in the middle of the Greek Peloponnese.

ARCHYTAS   A mathematician and philosopher of the Pythagorean school who flourished in Tarentum c. 400 B.C.

ARCTURUS   A constellation setting in October.

ARGIVES   Literally, men of Argos. Used loosely in heroic times to mean Greeks in general.

ARGO   The ship of the Argonauts (see Jason).

ARGONAUTS   See Jason.

ARGOS   City in the Argolid plain south of Corinth.

ASSARACUS   An ancient Trojan king.

ATHENE   See Pallas Athene.

ATLAS   A Giant who, for his part in the rebellion against the gods, was condemned to hold up the sky. Doing this, he became identified with the Atlas mountains in North Africa.

ATRIDES   Sons of Atreus, i.e. Agamemnon and Menelaus.

ATTALUS   Attalus III of Pergamum (d. 133 B.C.) was a byword for wealth, and unexpectedly bequeathed all his possessions to the Roman people.

AUFIDUS   The largest river in Apulia.

AULON   A valley near Tarentum.

AUSONIA   Land of the Ausones in Italy.

AUSTER   A south wind.

AVENTINE   One of the Seven Hills of Rome.

AVERNUS   This lake (still called Lago Averno) was thought to be one of the entrances to the underworld. It was never visited by birds (hence its Greek name: a-ornos).

BACCHANTES   Frenzied female worshippers of Bacchus (Dionysus).

BACCHUS    God of wine and ecstasy. There was a notorious cult of Dionysus (Bacchus) in Thrace.

BAIAE    A favoured seaside resort in Campania, just north of the Bay of Naples.

BANDUSIA    The spring near Horace's Sabine farm addressed in III.13.

BANTIA    A town in Apulia.

BELLEROPHON    Grandson of Sisyphus. At the court of Proetus, king of Argos, he repelled the queen's advances, so she denounced him. Proetus thereupon sent Bellerophon to the king of Lycia bearing a letter requesting his own death. Bellerophon was duly set various tasks (including slaying the Chimaera) likely to kill him: he performed them all and married the king's daughter.

BERECYNTIAN    This adjective is used to denote wind instruments of the type(s) used in the worship of Cybele (or Dindymene, q.v.) on Mount Berecyntus in Phrygia.

BIBULUS    M. Calpurnius Bibulus, consul in 59 B.C. with Julius Caesar.

BISTONES    A Thracian tribe.

BITHYNIA    An area to the west of Pontus renowned (like Pontus) for the quality of its timber.

BREUNI    An Alpine tribe.

BRISEIS    A beautiful slave-girl loved by Achilles and commandeered by Agamemnon. The resultant quarrel between the two heroes features largely in Homer's *Iliad*.

BUPALUS    A sculptor who produced a caricature of Hipponax, a poet of exceptional ugliness.


CADMUS    Legendary founder of Thebes. The site was guarded by a dragon which Cadmus killed, then sowed its teeth. A crop of warriors sprang up and fought and killed each other till only five were left. These five were the ancestors of the Theban nobility.

CAECUBAN    A highly regarded strong wine from the Caecuban district of Latium.

CAESAR    Augustus (called Octavian prior to 27 B.C.), first emperor of Rome (31 B.C.–A.D. 13), friend to Horace. He was deified after his death.

CALABRIA   A district in the south-east (the 'heel') of Italy.

CALES   A town in Campania, a wine-producing area.

CALLIOPE   The Muse of epic poetry.

CAMILLUS   An eminent man in the early history of Rome.

CANIDIA   A witch, unknown apart from the *Epodes* and *Satires* I.8.

CANTABRI, CANTABRIA   A warlike tribe and district in north-west Spain.

CAPITOL   The south-west summit of the Capitoline, one of the Seven Hills of Rome, on which stood the temple of Jupiter, Rome's special guardian.

CAPUA   Etruscan city in western Italy. It revolted from Rome during the war with Hannibal but was recaptured in 211 B.C.

CARPATHIAN SEA   The sea to the west of Crete.

CARTHAGE   North African city. Under their brilliant commander Hannibal, the Carthaginians nearly defeated and captured Rome. Carthage was finally destroyed by P. Scipio Africanus Minor in 146 B.C.

CASTALIA   A spring on Mt Parnassus sacred to the Muses.

CASTOR and POLLUX   Like their sister Helen (of Troy) they were children of Leda by Zeus (Jupiter) in the form of a swan. Among many exploits, they sailed with the Argonauts. After Castor's death they were allowed immortality on alternate days. They were later identified with the constellation Gemini, and protected travellers by sea.

CATILUS   Legendary founder of Tibur or father of three sons who jointly founded Tibur.

CATO   M. Porcius Cato (a) 'The elder', censor in 184 B.C., was famous for his austere and conservative way of life and for his attempts to impose it on others.

(b) 'The younger', great-grandson of the above, fought with Pompey in the republican cause against Julius Caesar, and killed himself after his side's defeat at Thapsus in 46 B.C.

CECROPS   Legendary first king of Athens.

CENSORINUS   C. Marcius Censorius, consul in 8 B.C.

CENTAURS   A legendary Thessalian race. They were human down to the waist, but there merged into horses. (See also Lapiths.)

CEOS   The island where the Greek lyric poets Simonides and Bacchylides were born.

CERBERUS   The dog who guarded the entrance to the underworld. He is usually credited with three heads, but sometimes with as many as a hundred.

CERES   The goddess of corn, identified with the Greek Demeter. The rites of her worship were meant to be kept secret by the initiated.

CHARON   The infernal ferryman whose employment was to carry the shades of the dead across the river Styx, so that they could gain admittance to the underworld.

CHARYBDIS   A fabled and deadly whirlpool located in the Straits of Messina.

CHIMAERA   A fire-breathing monster with a lion's head, goat's body and serpent's tail. It was defeated and killed by the hero Bellerophon riding the divine winged horse Pegasus.

CHIOS   An Aegean island from which Rome imported wine ('Chian').

CINARA   Horace's mistress: see Introduction, pp. 34–5.

CIRCE   An enchantress who detained Ulysses on his voyage back to Ithaca after the Trojan War. She turned his companions into swine, but changed them back into men after Ulysses had become her lover.

CLAUDIUS (CLAUDIAN)   The Claudian family was interrelated with Augustus' (the Julian) family. Claudius here usually denotes Tiberius, elder stepson of Augustus, later emperor.

CLIO   The Muse of history.

COCYTUS   One of the four rivers of the underworld.

CODRUS   The legendary last king of Athens who saved his people from the Dorian invaders by courting death when the oracle told him that Athens would be captured if his life was spared.

COLCHIS (COLCHIAN, COLCHIC)   Colchis, near the Black Sea, was the home of the sorceress-queen Medea, and was popularly associated with witchcraft and poison generally.

CONCANI   A tribe in north-west Spain.

CORVINUS   M. Valerius Messalla Corvinus, a general of Augustus; patron of Tibullus and other poets. He visits Horace in III.21.

CORYBANTES   See Dindymene.

COS   A Greek island noted for its fine silks.

COTISO   A Dacian commander defeated by Crassus in 30 B.C.

COTYTTO   A Thracian goddess whose mysteries apparently involved a degree of licence.

CRAGUS   A mountain in Lycia.

CRASSUS   M. Licinius Crassus, member of the first Triumvirate with Caesar and Pompey; campaigned in the east, but his army was defeated at Carrhae in Mesopotamia by the Parthians in 53 B.C.: the survivors settled among their captors.

CUPID   Son of Venus. Sometimes a figure of real power; sometimes a mischievous boy; sometimes pluralized into mere putti.

CURIUS   An eminent man in the early history of Rome.

CYCLADES   A group of small islands round Delos in the Aegean sea.

CYCLOPES   Servants of Vulcan. They manufactured Jupiter's thunderbolts.

CYLLENE   A mountain in Arcadia on which Mercury was born (hence Cyllenean lyres, because they are sacred to Mercury, their inventor).

CYNTHIA   Another name for Diana.

CYPRUS (CYPRIAN)   This island played an important part in ship-building and trade. It was also associated with Venus, since according to one legend she was first washed ashore at Paphos in Cyprus.

CYRUS   (a) Head of the Persian royal house in the sixth century B.C., from whom the Parthians claimed descent.

(b) Unknown lover(s) in I.17 and I.33.

CYTHEREA   Venus, so called because according to legend she was born from the sea near the island of Cythera.


DACIANS   A tribe allied to the Thracians. Their territory was situated in what is now Romania.

DAEDALUS   Fabulous architect and inventor who built the labyrinth at Knossos in which the Minotaur lived. He contrived wings from feathers and wax so that he and his son Icarus might escape from Crete.

DAMOCLES   The tyrant Dionysius I of Syracuse was called the happiest of men by one Damocles. Dionysius invited the flatterer to know the happiness of a king – a dinner at which a sword was suspended by a single horse-hair directly over the guest.

DANAË   Acrisius, king of Argos, was warned by an oracle that the son of his daughter Danaë would kill him. He therefore shut her up in a 'brazen tower', but Zeus (Jupiter) succeeded in visiting her in the form of a shower of gold. Their son, Perseus, killed Acrisius accidentally in a discus-throwing competition.

DANAUS   According to legend Danaus had fifty daughters and his brother Aegyptus had fifty sons. Aegyptus and his sons favoured the obvious solution of fifty simultaneous weddings. Danaus reluctantly agreed, but ordered his daughters to kill their husbands on the wedding night: all but one (Hypermnestra) obeyed. In the underworld the forty-nine murderesses were condemned forever to strive to fill jars with water – but as fast as the liquid was poured in, it vanished through the bottoms of the vessels, which remained dry.

DARDANIAN   Trojan.

DAUNIA (DAUNUS)   Apulia, the region in south-east Italy where Horace was born. Sometimes called Daunia on account of its mythological king Daunus.

DEIPHOBUS   A Trojan warrior, Hector's brother.

DELOS   The island where Apollo and Diana were born. 'Delian' wreaths were of laurel (or 'bays'), sacred to Apollo.

DELPHI   The site of the most important oracle in Greece. Apollo's oracles were given through a young priestess, the Pythia, and translated by the priests in charge.

DIANA   Goddess associated with woodlands, hunting, women, childbirth, and (through identification with the Greek Artemis) the moon and chastity. She also had a 'dark' aspect (whom the Greeks called Hecate) associated with witchcraft.

DINDYMENE   Cybele, the great mother-goddess of Phrygia, worshipped in ecstatic sacrificial rites. Her legendary priests were the Corybantes.

DIONE   The mother of Venus.

DIONYSUS   Bacchus.

DIRCE   A spring near Thebes – and thus near the birthplace of Pindar.

DOG-DAYS (DOG-STAR)   The Dog-days, i.e. the days of the Dog-star (Canicula), were usually reputed the hottest.

**DRUSUS**   Nero Claudius Drusus, stepson of Augustus: younger brother of Tiberius (later emperor); died in Germany in 9 B.C.

**EDONIANS**   A Thracian tribe reputed to be drunkards.

**EPHESUS**   Ionian city where there was a famous temple of Diana.

**ERYMANTHUS**   A mountain in Arcadia.

**ESQUILINE**   One of the Seven Hills of Rome. Part of it lay outside the walls and was used as a common burial-ground for the poorest paupers.

**EUROPA**   Daughter of Agenor, king of Tyre. Jupiter desired her and, in the guise of a white bull, carried her off on his back across the sea to Crete.

**EURUS**   The east wind.

**EUTERPE**   The Muse of flute-playing.

**FABRICIUS**   An eminent man in the early history of Rome.

**FALERNIAN**   Falernus was a district in Campania. Falernian wine was strong and highly prized.

**FATES**   There were three Fates. The first assigned each person's destiny; the second span the thread of his life; the third cut it at his death.

**FAUNUS**   The Italian shepherd-god; identified with Pan.

**FORENTUM**   A town in Apulia.

**FORMIAE**   A town in Latium (the region about Rome). It gave its name to a highly regarded wine.

**FURIES**   Supernatural, vengeful females who harried the guilty.

**GADES**   Cadiz.

**GAETULIA**   A North African territory adjoining Numidia.

**GALAESUS**   A river near Tarentum, the Spartan colony on the 'heel' of Italy.

**GANYMEDE**   A beautiful boy carried off by an eagle to be Zeus' (Jupiter's) cupbearer and catamite.

**GARGANUS**   (Monte Gargano)   A mountain ridge in Apulia.

**GELONI**   A nomadic Scythian tribe.

**GENITALIS**   'Bringer of birth'. Mentioned in the Centennial Hymn; the title is not found elsewhere.

**GETAE**   A Thracian tribe.

**GIANTS**   Sons of Heaven and Earth (Uranus and Ge). They

rebelled against Zeus (Jupiter), but were defeated and buried beneath mountains and volcanoes. Often identified or confused with the Titans.

GRATIA    One of the three Graces.

GROSPHUS    Pompeius Grosphus, mentioned as an honest friend in *Epistles* I.12.22, and known to be a Sicilian.

GYAS    A Giant.


HAEDUS    'The kid': a constellation rising in October.

HANNIBAL    The brilliant Carthaginian commander who brought his army (with elephants) over the Alps in 221 B.C., advanced through northern Italy and nearly captured Rome itself. He then campaigned in Italy for sixteen years.

HASDRUBAL    Younger brother of Hannibal. Defeated by C. Claudius Nero at the Italian river Metaurus in 207 B.C.

HEBRUS    (a) A Thracian river.
            (b) Neobule's (unknown) lover in III.12.

HECTOR    Eldest son of Priam king of Troy. Trojan hero of Homer's *Iliad*.

HELEN    Wife of Menelaus, king of Sparta. Her abduction by Paris, son of Priam (king of Troy) was the proximate cause of the Trojan war. Her father was Zeus (Jupiter) in the form of a swan, her mother Leda. Like her brothers Castor and Pollux, she was hatched from an egg.

HELICON    A mountain in Boeotia, sacred to the Muses.

HERCULES    One of the greatest mythological heroes, famous for his Twelve Labours.

HESPER    The evening star.

HESPERIA    Italy. (Hesperian: western, Italian.)

HIPPOLYTE    See Peleus.

HIPPOLYTUS    Son of Theseus, king of Athens. He was fanatically celibate and worshipped only Artemis (Diana). Phaedra, his stepmother, who desired him, in her fury contrived his violent death.

HYADES    A constellation of seven stars.

HYDASPES    A tributary of the Indus.

HYDRA    A many-headed monster. Its destruction was the second of Hercules' Twelve Labours. His difficulty was that as one head was cut off, two others grew.

HYLAEUS  A Centaur.

HYMETTUS  A mountain in Attica, famous to this day for its honey.

HYPERBOREAN  'Beyond the north'; this adjective denotes an imaginary region conceived of as an earthly paradise.

IAPIX  A west wind.

ICARUS (ICARIA)  Son of Daedalus, who made him wings of feathers and wax. Icarus flew too near the sun; the wax melted, he fell and drowned, and Daedalus buried him on the island known thereafter as Icaria. Likewise the eastern Aegean became the Icarian sea.

ICCIUS  In *Epistles* I.12 he is the steward of Agrippa's estates in Sicily. Otherwise unknown.

IDOMENEUS  The king of Crete who fought for the Greeks at Troy.

ILIA  Rhea Silvia was the mother (Mars was the father) of Romulus and Remus. She was a Vestal Virgin and the daughter of Numitor, king of Alba Longa. Later she was also called Ilia ('the Trojan', from *Ilium*, Troy), and was said to be the daughter of Aeneas, so as to fit in with the preferred legend of the origin of Rome.

ILITHYIA  A Greek goddess of childbirth.

ILIUM  Troy.

ILLYRIA  A part of what we now know as Yugoslavia.

INACHUS  Legendary first king of Argos.

IOLCOS  A part of Thessaly, notorious for witchcraft. The home of Jason.

ITYS  Tereus, king of Thrace married Procne (daughter of Pandion, king of Athens) and subsequently raped her sister Philomela and cut out her tongue. Philomela told Procne what had happened by weaving the message into a tapestry. In revenge the two women killed Itys, the son of Tereus and Procne, and served up his flesh to his father. Tereus pursued the sisters, but the gods intervened and turned all three into birds, Tereus becoming a hoopoe (a royal bird), Procne a nightingale and Philomela a swallow. (The details of the myth vary considerably from one source to another.)

IXION  A king of the Lapiths who tried to rape Juno, Jupiter's queen, and was consequently bound to a perpetually turning wheel in the underworld.

JASON    Son of Aeson, king of Iolcos in Thessaly. He assembled the heroic Argonauts and set out with them to fetch the Golden Fleece. He succeeded with the help of Medea. She also helped him at Colchis to carry out the task set by King Aeëtes (her father): to yoke a pair of fire-breathing bulls and sow dragon's teeth.

JOVE    See Jupiter.

JUBA (II)    King of Numidia during Horace's lifetime.

JUGURTHA    A king of Numidia; after many Roman victories in North Africa, Jugurtha was killed in 104 B.C.

JULUS    See Antonius.

JUNO    Queen of heaven, wife and sister of Jupiter.

JUPITER (JOVE)    King (or father) of the gods; especial guardian of Rome.

LAMIA    In III.17 probably L. Aelius Lamia, city prefect much later, in A.D. 32.

LAMUS    Legendary king of the Laestrygonians; mentioned in *Odyssey* 10.

LANUVIUM    A hill in Latium alongside the Appian Way.

LAOMEDON    An early king of Troy who employed Apollo and Poseidon (Neptune) to build the walls of his city, and then refused to pay them.

LAPITHS    A primitive Thessalian tribe who fought and won a famous drunken battle against the Centaurs at the wedding of Pirithous and Hippodamia.

LARES    Spirits of the dead, worshipped at crossroads and in the home as guardian deities – 'household gods'.

LATIUM    The district of Italy where Rome is situated.

LATONA    The mother (Jupiter was the father) of Apollo and Diana.

LENAEAN    'God of wine', Greek epithet of Dionysus (Bacchus).

LEO    A star rising in July.

LESBOS (LESBIAN)    The island of Lesbos was the home of Alcaeus and Sappho, the Greek lyric poets whom Horace regarded as his models, and whose characteristic metres he adapted to the Latin language in his Odes.

LETHE   One of the four rivers of the underworld. To drink its water was to obliterate memory.

LIBER   Italian god of wine-making, identified with Bacchus.

LIBITINA   Goddess of death.

LICINIUS   A. Terentius Varro Murena Licinius, brother of Proculeius and of Maecenas' wife Terentia; consul in 23 B.C.

LICYMNIA   Pseudonym for Terentia, wife of Maecenas.

LIRIS   A river in Latium.

LOLLIUS   M. Lollius, consul in 21 B.C. Defeated by the Sygambri in 17 B.C. on the Rhine frontier. Though accused of bribery and rapacity, he remained a friend of Augustus.

LUCERIA   A town in Apulia famous for its wool.

LUCINA   The name of Juno in her capacity of goddess of childbirth.

LUCRETILIS   A mountain near Horace's Sabine farm.

LUCRINUS   A lake near Naples. Its oysters were considered a delicacy.

LUNA   'The moon', Diana.

LYCAEUS   A mountain in Arcadia.

LYCAMBES   Though he had promised to do so, Lycambes refused to give his daughter in marriage to the poet Archilochus, who avenged himself in such bitter lampoons on Lycambes that the latter hanged himself.

LYCIA   A territory in Asia Minor to the south of Troy. It sent troops to assist Troy in the war against the Greeks.

LYCURGUS   A king of Thrace who opposed the entry of Dionysus (Bacchus) into his territory. The god punished him with madness and death.

LYDIA   A territory in Asia Minor.


MAECENAS   C. Maecenas, diplomat and personal friend of Augustus. Patron of Horace (also of Virgil, Propertius and others), to whom he gave his Sabine estate.

MAEVIUS   Unknown victim of Horace's invective in epode 10 – possibly the poetaster attacked by Virgil in *Eclogues* 3.90.

MANES   Deified shades of the dead.

MANLIUS    L. Manlius Torquatus, consul in 65 B.C., the year of Horace's birth.

MARCELLUS    The family of the Marcelli was distinguished from the Punic wars onward. One Marcellus was an eminent general against Hannibal. Another was the son-in-law of Augustus.

MARICA    A local goddess worshipped in the marshlands at the mouth of the Liris, a river in Latium.

MARS    God of war; father of Romulus.

MARSI (MARSIANS)    A central Italian tribe; noted soldiers, they rebelled against Rome in the Social War of 91 or 90–88 B.C.

MASSAGETAE    A Scythian tribe.

MASSIC    A highly regarded wine.

MATINE    Matinum was a coastal district of Apulia.

MEDE    Parthian.

MEDEA    Daughter of Aeetes, king of Colchis; a witch. She helped Jason win the Golden Fleece, and then returned with him to Iolcos, his home. After further vexations, the couple fled to Corinth. There Jason abandoned Medea for the daughter of King Creon. Medea killed the girl and her father with a poisoned robe and diadem, killed her own two children by Jason, and escaped in a dragon-drawn chariot first to Athens and then to Asia.

MELPOMENE    Strictly the Muse of tragedy and dirges, sometimes of poetry in general.

MENELAUS    King of Sparta. The abduction of his wife Helen by Paris was the proximate cause of the Trojan War, in which Menelaus participated.

MERCURY    Messenger of the gods; escort of the dead; patron of travellers and thieves; inventor of the lyre.

MERIONES    The charioteer of Idomeneus, king of Crete, at the siege of Troy.

METAURUS    The Italian river where Hasdrubal was defeated by C. Claudius Nero in 207 B.C. (This was the first Roman victory over the Carthaginians after a series of defeats.)

METELLUS    Q. Caecilius Metellus, consul in 60 B.C.

MINERVA    Goddess of war and domestic crafts, identified with Pallas Athene.

MINOS    Legendary king of Crete; son of Zeus (Jupiter); one of the three judges of the underworld.

MITYLENE   A city on the island of Lesbos.

MONAESES   A Parthian general.

MURENA   See Licinius.

MYCENAE   A city in Argos.

MYGDON   A prince of Phrygia.

MYRMIDONS   A bellicose Thessalian tribe who accompanied Achilles to the Trojan War.


NAIADS   River Nymphs.

NEPTUNE   The god of the sea.

NEREIDS   Sea Nymphs, daughters of Nereus.

NEREUS   A sea-god; father of the Nereids, including Thetis, mother of Achilles.

NERO(S)   Stepson(s) of Augustus: Tiberius (later emperor) and Drusus (who died in Germany in 9 B.C.)

NESSUS   Deianira, wife of Hercules, asked the Centaur Nessus to carry her over a river. He assaulted her and was shot by Hercules. Dying, he gave Deianira his bloody shirt, telling her it was a lovecharm. Years later when Hercules fell in love with another woman, Deianira sent him this shirt. He put it on and was seared, and killed himself (on a pyre) to end his agony. Then Deianira, too, committed suicide.

NESTOR   King of Pylos. He played an important part in the Greek campaign against Troy as adviser and 'elder statesman'.

NIOBE   Daughter of Tantalus and mother of fourteen children, seven of each sex. She boasted that she was superior to Latona. In retribution all her children were killed by Apollo and Diana, the offspring of Latona.

NIPHATES   A river or mountain in Armenia.

NIREUS   A hero said in the *Iliad* to be the most handsome of the Greeks.

NORICUM   A region between the Danube and the Alps famed for the high quality of its steel.

NOTUS   South wind associated with storms.

NUMA   Numa Pompilius, Romulus' immediate successor as king of Rome.

NUMANTIA   A town in Spain captured by P. Scipio Africanus after a siege lasting eight years.

NUMIDIA     A North African country to the south and south-west of Carthage; later a Roman province.

NYMPHS     Semi-divine women, tutelary spirits and personifications of natural objects – trees, rivers, etc.

OLYMPUS     A mountain in Greece, home of the gods.

ORCUS (PLUTO)     God of the underworld.

ORICUS     A port in Epirus.

ORION     A Giant from Boeotia, a keen hunter. Diana killed him for assaulting her. He gave his name to a constellation which sets in early November, usually a time of stormy weather.

ORPHEUS     A marvellous singer and lyrist. Apollo (who was in some versions of the story his father) gave him a lyre with which he was able to charm wild beasts and make rocks and trees follow him. He descended into the underworld in an ill-fated attempt to save his wife Eurydice from death.

OTHO     L. Roscius Otho carried a law in 67 B.C. that the first fourteen rows in the Theatre (next to the 'orchestra' where senators sat) should be reserved for knights, and so on according to degree.

PACORUS     A Parthian royal prince and general. He defeated a Roman army in 40 B.C.

PACTOLUS     A river in Lydia, said to have sands of gold.

PACTUMEIUS     The name of a Roman family or clan (*gens*).

PAELIGNI     A tribe inhabiting a mountainous district in central Italy.

PALATINE     One of the Seven Hills of Rome.

PALINURUS     The steersman of Ulysses' (Odysseus') ship, who fell overboard and was drowned. A cape in south-west Italy bore his name.

PALLAS ATHENE     Patron goddess of Athens, identified by the Romans with Minerva.

PAN     An Arcadian god, patron of shepherds and herdsmen. He was sometimes conceived of as a man-goat hybrid, amorous towards both sexes, and was associated with piping (i.e. upon the 'Pan-pipes')

PANAETIUS     A celebrated Stoic philosopher of the second century B.C.

PAPHOS   See Cyprus.

PARCAE   The Fates (q.v.).

PARIS   A son of Priam, king of Troy. His abduction of Helen, wife of Menelaus king of Sparta, was the proximate cause of the Trojan War.

PARRHASIUS   A celebrated Ephesian painter who flourished about 400 B.C.

PARTHIA   An empire located to the south-west of the Caspian Sea. Perhaps the most feared and hated rival of Rome during Horace's lifetime.

PATARA   A place on the river Xanthus in Lycia (south of Troy) where Apollo had an oracle.

PAULUS   L. Aemilius Paulus was commander with Varro of the army defeated by the Carthaginians under Hannibal at Cannae in 216 B.C.

PAULUS MAXIMUS   Fabius Paulus Maximus, consul in 11 B.C.; a friend of Augustus and member of one of the oldest noble families.

PEGASUS   Divine winged horse. See Chimaera.

PELEUS   King of Thessaly, husband of Thetis and father of Achilles. He was slandered by a woman much as was Bellerophon, and left asleep on Mt Pelion to be eaten by wild beasts, but he survived with the aid of the Centaur Chiron.

PELOPS   King of Lydia. Tantalus was the father of Pelops who was the father of Atreus who was the father of Agamemnon and Menelaus.

PENATES   Divine guardians of the household stores – 'household gods'.

PENELOPE   The faithful wife of Ulysses. The lover in III.10 calls her 'frigid' because she resisted a multiplicity of suitors during her husband's prolonged absence (see Homer's *Odyssey*).

PENTHEUS   A king of Thebes who opposed the cult of Dionysus (Bacchus). The god's followers killed him; his palace was overthrown in an earthquake.

PHAETHON   Son of Apollo (Phoebus). He stole his father's sun-chariot, was unable to control it, and was burnt to death.

PHALANTHUS   The Spartan adventurer who founded Tarentum.

PHILIPPI   City in East Macedonia, site of the battle in 42 B.C. where Brutus and Cassius, the leaders of the republican faction, were defeated and killed by Octavian (later Augustus). Horace fought under Brutus' command. He refers to this in II.7.

PHOCAEA    Greek town in Asia Minor. The Phocaeans, being besieged in 534 B.C., decided to abandon their city and sank a lump of iron, vowing not to return until it floated to the surface.

PHOEBUS    'Shining one', Apollo.

PHRAATES (IV)    A king of Parthia who was deposed by his subjects, but regained the throne by murdering his usurper Tiridates.

PHTHIA    A town in Thessaly associated with Achilles.

PIERIA    A district on the northern side of Mt Olympus in Thessaly, the home of the Muses.

PINDAR    Greek lyric poet (518–438 B.C.) famous for his odes.

PIRITHOUS    King of the Lapiths. See also Theseus.

PLANCUS    L. Munatius Plancus, consul in 42 B.C., the year of the battle of Philippi; the addressee of I.7, he was alleged to have proscribed his brother.

PLEIADES    A constellation rising in May and setting in November; associated with rain and storms.

PLUTO (ORCUS)    God of the underworld.

POLLIO, C. ASINIUS    A contemporary and friend of Horace; a writer of tragedies (none are extant); senator, advocate, patron of literature. He undertook a history of the Civil Wars from the consulship of Metellus in 60 B.C. (the year of the first Triumvirate) to the battle of Philippi in 42 B.C. See IV.1.

POLLUX    See Castor.

POLYHYMNIA    The Muse of sacred song.

POMPEIUS    (?Varus) Horace's friend of II.7, otherwise unknown.

POMPILIUS    See Numa.

PONTUS    A region south of the Black Sea famous for its timber.

PORSENNA    Lars Porsenna, Etruscan king of Clusium.

PRAENESTE    A hill-town near Rome.

PRIAM    King of Troy at the time of its sack by the Greeks under Agamemnon.

PRIAPUS    God of gardens, many of which contained his statue, ithyphallic and grasping a sickle, to frighten birds and thieves.

PROCULEIUS    C. Proculeius Varro Murena divided his property between his brothers, who had lost theirs in the civil wars.

PROCYON    A star rising in July.

PROETUS  See Bellerophon.

PROMETHEUS  A Titan of early Greek legend. He created man out of clay, taught him the arts, and stole fire for him from heaven. He was punished by Zeus (Jupiter) by being chained to Mt Caucasus with an eagle continuously pecking at his liver.

PROSERPINA  Queen of the underworld.

PROTEUS  A sea-god who tended the 'flocks' of Neptune.

PUNIC  Carthaginian. The Poeni (whence Punic) were the Phoenicians who founded Carthage.

PYRRHA  She and her husband Deucalion were the sole human survivors of the great flood sent by Zeus (Jupiter).

PYRRHUS  (a) King of Epirus who invaded Italy. The greater part of his army was destroyed at Asculum (279 B.C.), though the victory was his (hence the expression 'Pyrrhic victory').

(b) Unknown addressee of III.20.

PYTHAGORAS  A Greek philosopher and mathematician who flourished about 530 B.C. He was a strict vegetarian, holding that in the course of purification souls transmigrated between animal and man through successive reincarnations.

PYTHIA(N)  See Delphi.


QUIRINUS  See Romulus.

QUIRITES  Roman citizens in full possession of their civil rights.


REGULUS  M. Atilius Regulus, Roman consul and general and national hero. His army was defeated by the Carthaginians in 255 B.C., and he and many of his men were captured. In 250 B.C. he was sent back to Rome on parole to arrange a peace. He advised Rome to continue the war, returned to Carthage, and was tortured and executed with the remainder of his army.

REMUS  Twin brother of Romulus, who killed him in a quarrel over seniority.

RHAETI (ANS)  An Alpine tribe.

RHODOPE  A mountain in Thrace.

RHOETUS  One of the Giants.

ROMULUS (QUIRINUS)  Son of Mars. The legendary founder and first king of Rome, he was said to have disappeared in a thunderstorm in a chariot drawn by Mars' horses.

SABAEA   A region of Arabia. An unsuccessful expedition was made into Arabia Felix (Sabaea) in 24 B.C.

SABELLIAN   The Sabellians were an Italian mountain tribe from which many witches seem to have originated.

SABINE   The Sabine people occupied a district just north of Rome, where (at Tibur) the farm that Maecenas gave to Horace was located.

SALAMIS   (a) Teucer's native Greek island; the Persian fleet was defeated off its shores in 480 B.C.

(b) Having been banished from this Salamis by his father for having 'allowed' his brother Ajax to die, Teucer founded a second Salamis in Cyprus.

SALII   'Jumpers'. The dancing priests of Mars.

SALLUSTIUS CRISPUS, C.   Friend of Augustus, nephew of the historian Sallust.

SAPPHO   Lyric poet of Lesbos (q.v.), fl. 600 B.C. Her celebration of homosexual love accounts for the modern term 'lesbian'.

SATURN   The ruler of the gods and heaven preceding and deposed by Jupiter.

SATYRS   Mythical goat-men hybrids, often highly sexed.

SCAMANDER   A river near Troy.

SCAURI   This family was often linked with the Fabii, Curii, and Fabricii as an example of old-fashioned morality. M. Aemilius Scaurus was consul in 115 and censor in 109 B.C.

SCOPAS   A celebrated Parian sculptor who flourished about 375 B.C.

SCYTHIANS   Inhabitants of Scythia, a region to the north of the Black Sea.

SERES   The Chinese, who were already in Horace's time organizing the silk trade to Parthia.

SESTIUS   Lucius Sestius, consul in 23 B.C.

SIBYL   A variously localized prophetess, e.g. the Campanian Sibyl at Cumae.

SIDONIANS   The Phoenicians, the sea-traders of antiquity.

SILVANUS   God of woodlands. (In epode 2, line 22, he is evidently identified with Terminus, god of boundary stones.)

SIMOIS   A river near Troy.

SISYPHUS   A king of Corinth who for his sins was condemned in the underworld to push a great rock up a hill, from which it continually rolled down.

SORACTE  (Monte Soratte)  A mountain some twenty-five miles north of Rome.

SPARTACUS  The gladiator who led the slave rebellion in 73–71 B.C. He was eventually captured by Crassus and crucified with many of his followers.

STESICHORUS  A Greek lyric poet who lived *c.* 600 B.C.

STHENELUS  Charioteer of the Greek hero Diomedes (Tydides) at the siege of Troy.

STYX  One of the four rivers of the underworld. Charon ferried the shades of the dead across the Styx so that they could gain admittance to the underworld.

SUBURA  A street of bad repute in Rome.

SYBARIS  A Greek colony in southern Italy which became a byword for luxurious living.

SYGAMBRI  A German tribe who defeated a Roman army under M. Lollius in 16 B.C., but sued for peace when they heard Augustus himself was marching against them.

SYRTES  Dangerous shoals off the coast of North Africa. Also the desert of the hinterland.


TAENARUS  A promontory of Laconia (Cape Matapan) where there was supposed to be an entrance to the underworld.

TANTALUS  The father of Pelops. A notorious sinner in myth, he was punished in the underworld by being stuck fast near food and water which receded when he tried to eat or drink.

TARENTUM  (Taranto)  A Spartan colony on the 'heel' of Italy.

TARQUIN(S)  The Etruscan noble family which provided two kings of early Rome. Tarquinius Superbus was the last of the kings of Rome; his fall in 510 B.C. led to the foundation of the Republic.

TARTARUS  A region of the underworld devoted to the punishment of evil.

TECMESSA  A Trojan princess whose father was killed by Ajax.

TELEGONUS  Legendary founder of Tusculum in Latium; a son of Ulysses and Circe; he killed his father by mistake.

TELEPHUS  (a) a king of the Mysians; Achilles wounded him with a spear, but then (as had been foretold by an oracle) healed him with rust from the same weapon.

(b) Unknown young man/men of I.13, III.19 and IV.11.

TEMPE   A beautiful valley in Thessaly.

TERMINUS   God of boundary stones.

TEUCER   A Greek hero at the siege of Troy; brother of Ajax. See also Salamis.

THALIA   The Muse of comedy.

THEBES   A Boeotian city; the scene of various Greek myths, including those of Cadmus and of Oedipus.

THESEUS   Legendary king of Athens, father of Hippolytus. With his friend Pirithous, he attempted to abduct Proserpina from the underworld. Pirithous was caught and put in chains.

THESSALY   A region,of northern Greece notorious for being only semi-civilized and for magical goings-on. See Centaurs, Lapiths and Peleus.

THETIS   A sea-goddess. Mother of Achilles by Peleus.

THRACE (THRACIANS)   A primitive region north of Greece. Horace habitually associates the Thracians with drunkenness, presumably on account of their cult of Dionysus (Bacchus), god of wine and ecstasy.

THYESTES   His own children were served up to him at a banquet given by his brother Atreus (father of Agamemnon and Menelaus), on whose house he laid a curse of revenge (cf. Aeschylus' *Oresteia*).

THYONEUS   An epithet of Bacchus.

TIBERIUS   The elder stepson of Augustus (the younger was Drusus); later emperor.

TIBULLUS   Albius Tibullus, elegiac poet, d. 19 B.C.; friend of Horace and Ovid; friend and protégé of M. Valerius Messalla Corvinus.

TIBUR   (Tivoli)   Town twenty miles north-east of Rome, near Horace's Sabine farm.

TIRIDATES (II)   Usurper to the throne of Parthia; in 30–29 B.C. a refugee in Syria, supported by Octavian (later Augustus).

TITANS   In early Greek legends gods or demi-gods; the children of Heaven and Earth (Uranus and Ge); often identified or confused with the Giants.

TITHONUS  A mortal who was granted eternal life – but not (owing to an oversight) eternal youth, so his doom was perpetual ageing.

TITYOS  A Giant who attempted to violate Latona and was killed by her children Apollo and Diana.

TORQUATUS  (a) Addressee of IV.7 and *Epistles* I.5, otherwise unknown.

(b) L. Manlius Torquatus – see Manlius.

TROILUS  A son of Priam, king of Troy; killed by Achilles in the Trojan War.

TULLUS  (a) Tullus Hostilius, third king of Rome.

(b) L. Vocatius Tullus, consul in 66 B.C.

TUSCULUM (Frascati)  A mountain town ten miles south-east of Rome founded by Telegonus, son of Ulysses and Circe.

TYDIDES  Son of Tydeus, i.e. Diomedes, a Greek warrior at the siege of Troy.

TYRE  Eastern Mediterranean city and sea-port famous for its woollen fabrics and its dyes.

ULYSSES (Odysseus)  Greek hero whose many adventures in the course of his return from Troy to his native Ithaca and his faithful wife Penelope form the subject of Homer's *Odyssey*.

USTICA  A valley (or perhaps a hill) near Horace's Sabine farm.

VALGIUS  C. Valgius Rufus, a member of Maecenas' circle of poets (cf. *Satires* I.10.81–2).

VENAFRUM  A town in Campania, famous for its olive-groves.

VENUS  Goddess of love.

VENUSIA (Venosa)  A town on the borders of Apulia and Lucania; Horace's birthplace.

VESPER (Hesper)  The evening star.

VESTA  Roman goddess of the hearth.

VINDELICI  Tyrolean tribe defeated by Tiberius and Drusus in 15 B.C.

VIRGIL  (a) Illustrious poet, author of the *Aeneid*, contemporary and friend of Horace.

(b) Unknown addressee of IV.12.

VULCAN  The blacksmith-god, husband of Venus.

VULTUR  A mountain in Apulia, near Venusia.

XANTHUS    The name of several rivers in Asia Minor – in IV.6
probably that in Lycia where Apollo had an oracle at Patara, on
its banks.

ZEPHYR    The west wind of spring.

# INDEX
# TO
# POEMS

## EPODES

| | | | |
|---|---|---|---|
| Altera iam teritur | 16 | Nox erat et caelo | 15 |
| At, o deorum | 5 | | |
| | | Parentis olim | 3 |
| Beatus ille | 2 | Petti, nihil me | 11 |
| Horrida tempestas | 13 | | |
| Iam iam efficaci | 17 | Quando repostum | |
| | | Caecubum | 9 |
| Ibis Liburnis | 1 | Quid immerentis hospites | 6 |
| Lupis et agnis | 4 | Quid tibi vis | 12 |
| | | Quo, quo, scelesti ruitis? | 7 |
| Mala soluta navis | 10 | | |
| Mollis inertia | 14 | Rogare longo | 8 |

## ODES

| | | | |
|---|---|---|---|
| Aeli vetusto | III.17 | Audivere, Lyce | IV.13 |
| Aequam memento | II.3 | | |
| Albi, ne doleas | I.33 | Bacchum in remotis | II.19 |
| Angustam amice | III.2 | Caelo supinas | III.23 |

Caelo tonantem            III.5
Cum tu, Lydia             I.13
Cur me querelis           II.17

Delicta maiorum           III.6
Descende caelo            III.4
Dianam tenerae            I.21
Diffugere nives           IV.7
Dive, quem proles         IV.6
Divis orte bonis          IV.5
Donarem pateras           IV.8
Donec gratus eram         III.9

Eheu fugaces              II.14
Est mihi nonum            IV.11
Et ture et fidibus        I.36
Exegi monumentum          III.30
Extremum Tanain           III.10

Faune, Nympharum          III.18
Festo quid potius die     III.28

Herculis ritu             III.14

Iam pauca aratro          II.15
Iam satis terris          I.2
Iam veris comites         IV.12
Icci, beatis              I.29
Ille et nefasto           II.13
Impios parrae             III.27
Inclusam Danaen           III.16
Intactis opulentior       III.24
Integer vitae             I.22
Intermissa, Venus         IV.1
Iustum et tenacem         III.3

Laudabunt alii            I.7
Lydia, dic, per omnis     I.8

Maecenas atavis edite     I.1
Martiis caelebs           III.8
Mater saeva Cupidinum     I.19
Mercuri, facunde          I.10

Mercuri – nam te          III.11
Miserarum est             III.12
Montium custos            III.22
Motum ex Metello          II.1
Musis amicus              I.26

Natis in usum             I.27
Ne forte credas           IV.9
Ne sit ancillae           II.4
Nolis longa ferae         II.12
Non ebur neque aureum     II.18
Non semper imbres         II.9
Non usitata               II.20
Non vides quanto          III.20
Nondum subacta            II.5
Nullam, Vare, sacra       I.18
Nullus argento            II.2
Nunc est bibendum         I.37

O crudelis adhuc          IV.10
O diva, gratum            I.35
O fons Bandusiae          III.13
O matre pulchra           I.16
O nata mecum              III.21
O navis, referent         I.14
O saepe mecum             II.7
O Venus, regina           I.30
Odi profanum vulgus       III.1
Otium divos               II.16

Parcius iunctas           I.25
Parcus deorum cultor      I.34
Pastor cum traheret       I.15
Persicos odi              I.38
Phoebe        Centennial
  silvarumque       Hymn
Phoebus volentem          IV.15
Pindarum quisquis         IV.2
Poscimur. Si quid         I.32

Quae cura patrum          IV.14

Qualem ministrum       IV.4
Quantum distet         III.19
Quem tu, Melpomene     IV.3
Quem virum aut heroa   I.12
Quid bellicosus        II.11
Quid dedicatum         I.31
Quid fles, Asterie     III.7
Quis desiderio         I.24
Quis multa gracilis    I.5
Quo me, Bacche, rapis  III.25

Rectius vives          II.10

Scriberis Vario        I.6
Septimi, Gades aditure II.6

Sic te diva            I.3
Solvitur acris hiems   I.4

Te maris et terrae     I.28
Tu ne quaesieris       I.11
Tyrrhena regum         III.29

Ulla si iuris          II.8
Uxor pauperis I byci   III.15

Velox amoenum          I.17
Vides ut alta          I.9
Vile potabis           I.20
Vitas inuleo           I.23
Vixi puellis nuper     III.26

# READ MORE IN PENGUIN

In every corner of the world, on every subject under the sun, Penguin represents quality and variety – the very best in publishing today.

For complete information about books available from Penguin – including Puffins, Penguin Classics and Arkana – and how to order them, write to us at the appropriate address below. Please note that for copyright reasons the selection of books varies from country to country.

**In the United Kingdom**: Please write to *Dept. EP, Penguin Books Ltd, Bath Road, Harmondsworth, West Drayton, Middlesex UB7 0DA*

**In the United States**: Please write to *Consumer Sales, Penguin Putnam Inc., P.O. Box 12289 Dept. B, Newark, New Jersey 07101-5289*. VISA and MasterCard holders call 1-800-788-6262 to order Penguin titles

**In Canada**: Please write to *Penguin Books Canada Ltd, 10 Alcorn Avenue, Suite 300, Toronto, Ontario M4V 3B2*

**In Australia**: Please write to *Penguin Books Australia Ltd, P.O. Box 257, Ringwood, Victoria 3134*

**In New Zealand**: Please write to *Penguin Books (NZ) Ltd, Private Bag 102902, North Shore Mail Centre, Auckland 10*

**In India**: Please write to *Penguin Books India Pvt Ltd, 11 Community Centre, Panchsheel Park, New Delhi 110017*

**In the Netherlands**: Please write to *Penguin Books Netherlands bv, Postbus 3507, NL-1001 AH Amsterdam*

**In Germany**: Please write to *Penguin Books Deutschland GmbH, Metzlerstrasse 26, 60594 Frankfurt am Main*

**In Spain**: Please write to *Penguin Books S. A., Bravo Murillo 19, 1° B, 28015 Madrid*

**In Italy**: Please write to *Penguin Italia s.r.l., Via Benedetto Croce 2, 20094 Corsico, Milano*

**In France**: Please write to *Penguin France, Le Carré Wilson, 62 rue Benjamin Baillaud, 31500 Toulouse*

**In Japan**: Please write to *Penguin Books Japan Ltd, Kaneko Building, 2-3-25 Koraku, Bunkyo-Ku, Tokyo 112*

**In South Africa**: Please write to *Penguin Books South Africa (Pty) Ltd, Private Bag X14, Parkview, 2122 Johannesburg*

# READ MORE IN PENGUIN

## A CHOICE OF CLASSICS

| | |
|---|---|
| Hesiod/Theognis | **Theogony/Works and Days/Elegies** |
| Hippocrates | **Hippocratic Writings** |
| Homer | **The Iliad** |
| | **The Odyssey** |
| Horace | **Complete Odes and Epodes** |
| Horace/Persius | **Satires and Epistles** |
| Juvenal | **The Sixteen Satires** |
| Livy | **The Early History of Rome** |
| | **Rome and Italy** |
| | **Rome and the Mediterranean** |
| | **The War with Hannibal** |
| Lucretius | **On the Nature of the Universe** |
| Martial | **Epigrams** |
| Ovid | **The Erotic Poems** |
| | **Heroides** |
| | **Metamorphoses** |
| | **The Poems of Exile** |
| Pausanias | **Guide to Greece** (in two volumes) |
| Petronius/Seneca | **The Satyricon/The Apocolocyntosis** |
| Pindar | **The Odes** |
| Plato | **Early Socratic Dialogues** |
| | **Gorgias** |
| | **The Last Days of Socrates (Euthyphro/ The Apology/Crito/Phaedo)** |
| | **The Laws** |
| | **Phaedrus** and **Letters VII and VIII** |
| | **Philebus** |
| | **Protagoras/Meno** |
| | **The Republic** |
| | **The Symposium** |
| | **Theaetetus** |
| | **Timaeus/Critias** |